America Works

America Works

The Exceptional
U.S. Labor Market

✺

Richard B. Freeman

A Russell Sage Foundation Centennial Volume

Russell Sage Foundation
New York

The Russell Sage Foundation

The Russell Sage Foundation, one of the oldest of America's general purpose foundations, was established in 1907 by Mrs. Margaret Olivia Sage for "the improvement of social and living conditions in the United States." The Foundation seeks to fulfill this mandate by fostering the development and dissemination of knowledge about the country's political, social, and economic problems. While the Foundation endeavors to assure the accuracy and objectivity of each book it publishes, the conclusions and interpretations in Russell Sage Foundation publications are those of the authors and not of the Foundation, its Trustees, or its staff. Publication by Russell Sage, therefore, does not imply Foundation endorsement.

Library of Congress Cataloging-in-Publication Data

Freeman, Richard B. (Richard Barry), 1943–
    America works : critical thoughts on the exceptional U.S. labor market / Richard B. Freeman.
        p. cm. — (A Russell Sage Foundation Centennial Volume)
    Includes bibliographical references and index.
    ISBN 978-0-87154-283-0 (HB)   978-0-87154-326-4 (PB)
    1. Labor market—United States.   I. Title.

    HD5724.F734 2007
    331.10973—dc22   2006038382

Text design by Suzanne Nichols.

RUSSELL SAGE FOUNDATION
112 East 64th Street, New York, New York 10065
10   9   8   7   6   5   4   3   2   1

This book is dedicated to colleagues and friends in labor economics, with whom I have shared and learned much. Thanks to our collective scholarship, the study of labor has moved from being a peripheral "weak" field in economics to one of the premier contributors to our knowledge of the economy. Because labor economics is data-driven, we have reached considerable agreement about how workers fare and how labor markets operate, irrespective of ideological views. But we often disagree about how to make the labor market work better for all persons. May this book contribute to that disagreement.

CONTENTS

About the Author

Richard B. Freeman is Herbert Ascherman Chair in Economics at Harvard University and director of the Labor Studies Program at the National Bureau of Economic Research. He is also Senior Research Fellow in Labour Markets at the London School of Economics' Centre for Economic Performance.

THE RUSSELL SAGE CENTENNIAL VOLUMES

America Works: Critical Thoughts on the Exceptional U.S. Labor Market
Richard B. Freeman

Categorically Unequal: The American Stratification System
Douglas S. Massey

Social Science for What? Philanthropy and the Social Question in a World Turned Rightside Up
Alice O'Connor

FOREWORD

On April 19, 2007, the Russell Sage Foundation will celebrate its centennial, 100 years to the day since Margaret Olivia Sage dedicated the foundation, in her husband's name, "to the improvement of social and living conditions in the United States of America." From the outset, social research played a key role in the foundation's mission—both by providing vivid descriptions of the social problems that called out for reform in a newly industrialized, urbanized America and by assessing the effectiveness of the foundation's early programs designed to improve the lot of the disadvantaged. As the foundation's enterprise matured after World War II, the Russell Sage trustees realized that to better serve the emerging mass society social science would require significant development—in its analytic tools, its sources of data, and its theoretical capacities. Accordingly, the trustees decided that a foundation the size of RSF could contribute to the general social welfare most effectively by investing directly in the development and application of social science. This has been the foundation's unique objective ever since.

Over the past sixty years, the foundation has sought to shape and strengthen the social sciences in a wide variety of ways. It has invested in new disciplines, among them the sociology of medicine and law, and a new brand of economics based less on presumed rationality and more on evidence about how economic decisions are actually made. It has pushed to create new sources of social data, such as the General Social Survey, and to improve the analysis of existing data sources, principally by means of its long-standing analysis of social trends revealed by the U.S. Census. Russell Sage has also worked to support and disseminate promising new methodologies, such as statistical techniques for synthesizing multiple research studies of a given social policy or program to achieve more reliable generalizations about what works.

The foundation's recent activities have sustained its traditional aims of bringing social science more effectively to bear on describing social problems and analyzing the causes and consequences of social change. RSF has developed research programs on the social consequences of changing gender roles in the wake of the civil rights movement, on the vexing persistence of poverty and the rise of economic inequality in the United States over the past three decades, on the declining fortunes of minority workers in the inner-city economies of the 1980s and early 1990s, and on the tectonic shifts in the U.S. labor market since the early 1980s that have put workers with limited education and bargaining power at such a distinct and growing disadvantage. Russell Sage has also devoted substantial attention to understanding the social consequences of recent demographic change. The foundation's fifteen-year program of research on the continuing wave of immigration to the United States provides a rich source of information about the impact the new immigrants are having on the country and the problems that immigrants and their children face as they try to make their way in American society. A related research program has addressed the changes in American life brought on by the increased diversity of the U.S. population—from the growing complexity of relations between racial and ethnic groups to the problems that American institutions encounter as they attempt to accommodate a more diverse citizenry.

The Russell Sage Foundation's hundredth birthday offers a unique moment to pause and take stock of this work, even as the enterprise continues. The three volumes commissioned for the centennial illustrate and reflect upon the use of social science to deepen our understanding of American life. They do not recapitulate the work of the foundation. They seek instead to push the work ahead. Over its long history, Russell Sage has struggled repeatedly to understand the social costs of the rough and tumble American labor market, the systemic roots of persistently high levels of inequality in the United States, and the political difficulties of establishing an effective role for social research in the formation of social policy.

The three centennial volumes take up these themes with innovative and provocative arguments that demonstrate again the power of social research to move debate beyond conventional wisdom, to give society fresh ways to see itself, and to recommend new strategies for improving national life. No doubt these arguments will provide rich grounds for debate. But since social science is, after all, a continuing contest founded on a shared commitment to honest evidence and reasoned argument, that is just as it should be.

Eric Wanner
President
Russell Sage Foundation

INTRODUCTION

In 1984 the American Economics Association sent a delegation of economists to the Soviet Union for scientific discussion with Soviet economists. It was the final meeting in a series of cultural exchanges at a time when the Cold War was heating up. The trip was made in summer, but in terms of intellectual discourse, Moscow was as cold and dark as Mordor. At lunch the head of the Soviet delegation reminded us that the Soviet Union had enough nuclear weapons to destroy the United States many times over, including President Reagan's Hollywood and Disneyland.

My job was to talk about the U.S. labor market. I criticized the United States for rising inequality; unemployment that had hit double digits in the 1981 recession; declining unionization; reduced company provision of defined-benefit pensions; the stalled advance of black Americans; limited gains in earnings for women; and slow productivity and real wage growth. I saw the United States as losing ground to other advanced economies. Japan, whose labor market and economic institutions were very different from those in the United States, was challenging American firms in automobiles, steel, and high-tech. Advanced Europe, which also had very different institutions, had adjusted better to the 1970s oil shock.

My biggest concern was that the distribution of earnings in the United States was bifurcating. There were more jobs and higher pay at the top of the earnings distribution and also at the bottom of the earnings distribution. The result was fewer middle-class workers. The average hourly earnings of the production and nonsupervisory workers who made up most of the U.S. workforce were trending downward, in a sharp break with U.S. economic history. Crime was high. Social pathologies were destroying inner cities. Homeless people, whom I had always associated with impoverished India or hobos during the Great Depression, were found on the streets of big

1

cities. The Reagan administration's tax cut targeted at the rich was to me the wrong way to solve the country's economic problems. I was tough on the U.S. labor market and economy.

The KGB agent who accompanied the Soviet delegation liked my criticisms. He offered me a piece of Russian chewing gum. Maybe Comrade Konstantin Chernenko, the chairman of the Politburo, would use my statistics the next time he denounced the United States. But Comrade Chernenko was not as sharp as Comrade Yuri Andropov (the previous chairman, who came from the KGB). Was I interested in future trips to Moscow as a friend of the KGB? I could stay in the Friendship Hotel (a decrepit, overcrowded slum dwelling filled with spy cameras and aged babushkas), drink vodka and eat caviar (with bloated Party apparatchiks), and go to Red Square to watch the May Day parade (of weapons designed to destroy me, my family and friends, Hollywood, and Disneyland). I could denounce the Reagan administration to my heart's content.

Shades of Maxwell Smart and KAOS![1] I was critical of the United States because I wanted the country to do better, not because I sympathized with the decaying "Evil Empire." (President Reagan's words rang true to me after that visit.) Wondering if other Russians thought that Andropov was a better leader than Chernenko, I repeated the comment to a Russian economist and watched the man's face turn ash white and his trembling hand spill the vodka as he backed across the room as quickly as he could. Criticize the leader and you just might end up in Moscow's notorious Lubyanka Prison. I was ecstatic when the airplane taking our delegation back to civilization took off from Moscow, leaving behind armed guards at the airport, bookstores filled with Marx and Lenin, and horrid chewing gum. When we landed in Helsinki, I thought it was Paris.

Some of the weaknesses in the U.S. job market and economy that troubled me in Moscow over two decades ago have lessened. In the late 1990s boom, employment rose to unprecedented levels relative to the population of working age, and the rate of productivity advance accelerated. Women made huge gains in the labor market, and crime fell greatly, though that decline may have been the result of the number of persons imprisoned rising to levels unprecedented in any free society.

Other problems, however, got worse. Inequality is now at Third World levels. Real wages have continued to stagnate. The U.S. union movement has weakened and split. And new problems have arisen that I never imagined would plague the United States. While the number of crimes committed by normal citizens has fallen, a wave of crime and amoral greed has engulfed the CEOs of major corporations, harming workers and shareholders alike. The demand for labor has shifted toward highly skilled "superstars" and away from ordinary workers, exacerbating inequality. Most important, globalization is creating a single world labor market in which multinational firms shift jobs from Americans to low-wage workers in developing countries, creating insecurity and uncertainty in the United States about the economic future. Historically, American labor scholars have looked inward to examine U.S. laws and institutions, paying scant regard to the rest of the world, but that traditional approach will not do in the twenty-first century. Globalization has brought the world to the United States—through immigration, trade, capital flows, and the Internet—with huge consequences for American workers and firms.

The United States has an exceptional labor market. With less institutional regulation than is found in any other major advanced country, it relies on decentralized wage setting to determine pay and provides workers with lower safety nets to deal with unemployment, disability, and health problems. It gives managers great rewards and power. Historians and political scientists often write about "American exceptionalism"—the extent to which the frontier, openness to immigration, high religiosity, and rejection of European-style class politics has made the United States different from other advanced capitalist countries.[2] Economists examine how the U.S. labor market produces different outcomes than those in Europe or Japan.[3] Some see the U.S. market as the nearest thing to the "invisible hand" market of economic theory, and a main reason for U.S. economic success.

This book does not join in this sanguine view of the U.S. economic model. I take a more critical view of the performance of the U.S. labor market. The triumph of market capitalism and the collapse of the Soviet bloc have not blunted my belief that the U.S. labor system can do better. I am critical of the U.S. model, as I was in Moscow, because it has weaknesses that harm workers but can be remedied, I believe, without reducing growth and productivity. I recognize that there are powerful market and nonmarket forces that act to increase inequality in the United States, from technological change that favors the more skilled to globalization, which places U.S. workers in competition with lower-wage workers elsewhere in the world. But these forces are not all-powerful. The country can strengthen the market forces and institutions that favor ordinary workers. It can adjust to globalization in ways that will yield better outcomes for working citizens. My critical view of the U.S. labor market is not one of doom and gloom but one that sees the opportunity to do better.

Part of the historic success of the United States comes from its reliance on markets. But part of its success also has to do with how government and institutions operate and the ways in which the country has historically supplemented or amended market outcomes. The United States was the first country to develop mass higher education. The federal government's investments in research and development have produced innovations such as the Internet that have spurred the private economy as well as advances in medicine that elongate lives. The government has battled against discrimination in the job market, used tax and transfer policies to provide social security for the elderly, enacted laws and rules that reduce occupational injuries and deaths, and set up a legal system for workers to unionize through secret ballot elections. Some of these policies have worked well. Some have not. But the same is true of markets. Sometimes markets work well. Sometimes they do not. The most sophisticated market in capitalism, the financial market, fluctuates wildly for reasons no one understands, not even Warren Buffett or George Soros. Without a powerful Securities and Exchange Commission regulating financial transactions, Wall Street would turn into a fraudulent casino. The differences between the ways in which stock and currency markets

4

work in reality and abstract models of perfectly efficient markets have led financial economists to devote more resources to "behavioral economics," studies that seek to understand the flaws and foibles of real markets. Labor economics has always been behavioral economics.

The first eight chapters of this book are about the functioning of U.S. labor markets and the resulting successes and failures. These chapters are based on the scientific analyses of economists with widely different perspectives and ideologies. In the lingo of social science, they are "positive economics." In the lingo of Joe Friday from the old *Dragnet* TV show, these chapters are about the facts, m'am, just the facts.[4] Where economists and other social scientists disagree about the processes that have generated the facts, I give you both sides—my (hopefully) correct view and the alternative view.

The last chapter moves to normative issues. I lay out how I believe the country can restructure the labor market and supplement market solutions to improve the well-being of ordinary workers. In contrast to recent policy debate, in which politicians and policy analysts often claim that whatever policies they favor—tax cuts for the rich, lower trade barriers, greater spending on education— make the economy better for everyone, I do not sell my policy prescriptions as "win-win" solutions. Almost all policies benefit some people—tax cuts for the rich benefit the rich, and reduced trade barriers benefit consumers of goods with lower tariffs—but those benefits may or may not trickle down or across to the rest of society. Most policies also create losers, usually indirectly—the tax cut to the rich may come at the expense of greater spending on social programs, reduced trade barriers often harm manufacturing firms and their workers—and it is disingenuous to claim otherwise. Even with the rare win-win policies, there are huge distributional issues: does the extra output go primarily to lower-income workers and their families or primarily to well-heeled professionals and executives?

My prescriptions are designed to make it easier for ordinary workers to advance their interests in the labor market. Given the extraordinary inequality in the U.S. job market, this must be done by shifting some national output from the super-wealthy to regular employees and reducing the control over the U.S. economy exerted by the super-wealthy. Sorry, Bill, Warren, George, and the rest of the billionaires on the *Forbes* "400 Richest Americans" list.[5] But more than anyone else, you know that a bit less for you and a bit more for the average American will do the country good—and will not inhibit your efforts to make your firms and investments succeed.

◈ CHAPTER 1 ◈

THE U.S. MARKET-DRIVEN LABOR SYSTEM

> Mirror, mirror on the wall, whose labor system is the most market-driven of all? Queen, among the major advanced economies, one stands apart from all the rest. The United States has the most market-driven wage and employment system by far.

More than any other advanced country, the United States relies on the competitive labor market to determine the well-being of workers and the living standards of their families. The collective bargaining institutions, government regulations, and social safety nets that capitalist economies use to constrain market forces and ensure a minimal level of economic well-being are weaker in the United States than in other high-income countries. As a result, working in this country is more important to the economic life of individuals than it is in the European Union (EU), Japan, or even America's kissing cousin, Canada. With limited unemployment insurance and other social protections, American workers cannot afford long spells of unemployment. With no national health insurance, American workers have to find an employer that offers insurance, have a spouse who is covered, or purchase insurance individually at costs far above those available to employees. With no national wage or benefit negotiations and limited union or other group activities in their workplaces, American workers have to find a job with an employer who pays decent wages and treats workers well.

In this chapter, I document that the United States is truly exceptional in its reliance on the labor market in determining economic outcomes. I do this by comparing quantitative measures of how the

United States and other advanced countries determine pay, provide social support, and regulate the labor market. Because all countries enact labor laws to protect workers, I focus on differences in how they implement these laws as well as on the de jure rules. Some readers may view the quantification as excessive. Why not just trust the mirror on the wall? Surely no one believes that the United States is less market-driven than the European Union? But quantification is necessary to assess whether the U.S. labor market stands apart *by enough* to explain the unique American employment and wage experiences, or whether we have to look more broadly at other societal differences.

Exceptional in Wage Setting and Social Insurance

The Fraser Institute in Vancouver, Canada, is a right-wing think tank devoted to market economics. Since the 1980s, the institute has produced "indices of economic freedom" for countries based on metrics for "personal choice, voluntary exchange coordinated by markets, freedom to enter and compete, and protection of persons and their property."[1] The Fraser index scales economies from 1 to 10, with higher scores reflecting greater dependence on markets as opposed to institutions. The index is made up of a set of sub-indices: for the government, legal structure, monetary policy, and free trade and for regulation of the labor market, credit markets, and business, taken separately.

The conservative orientation of the Fraser Institute affects how it defines economic freedom. It codes legal protection of property as a positive factor in economic freedom but codes legal protection of labor as a negative factor in economic freedom on the grounds that this restricts the ability of businesses to make decisions.[2] It regards government regulations and welfare state spending as lowering economic freedom, although these activities can limit monopoly power and expand the economic freedom of disadvantaged groups. The institute's measure is thus more of an index of the leeway that societies give to markets and business or capital than a broad measure of economic freedom. But nomenclature aside, the institute's

Figure 1.1   Advanced Countries Rated by Fraser Institute
Indices of Labor Market Regulation and the Role
of Government in the Economy, 2004

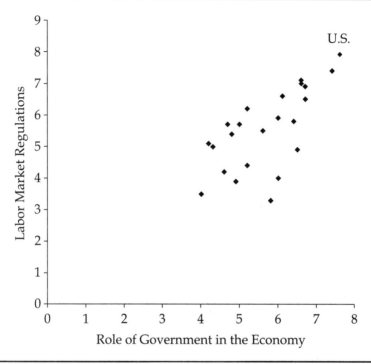

Source: Fraser Institute, "Economic Freedom of the World: 2006 Annual Report," table 1.3; available at http:www.freetheworld.com/2006/1EFW 2006ch1.pdf.
Note: The higher the value, the more market-oriented the country is.

indices are just the kind of measures to test the principal claim of this chapter.

Figure 1.1 shows the score of the United States and other advanced countries in two of the Fraser Institute's sub-indices of economic freedom: regulation of the labor market (along the vertical axis) and the role of the government in the economy (along the horizontal axis). A high score on an index means that the country is more market-oriented. The United States lies on the upper right-hand side of the figure. It has the highest score on the labor market scale and the second highest on the government scale. On both scales, the United States diverges statistically from the mean for the group.[3]

The Fraser Institute also scores countries by the market-friendliness of their policies toward trade, money, financial markets, and legal protection of property. On these indicators, the United States looks similar to the other countries. For instance, Sweden, which the Fraser Institute rates as having the lowest score in the role of government in the economy, owing to its high tax and spend policy, has a higher rating than the United States in legal protection of property. Germany, which gets the lowest score in the institute's measure of the labor market, has a higher rating than the United States in the institute's measure of free-trade policies. The United States is exceptional in its labor market and limited social intervention in worker outcomes, not in the other dimensions of a market economy.

Some readers may worry that the conservative orientation of the Fraser Institute biases its assessments of the market orientation of advanced countries. Maybe union leaders or persons with a liberal or progressive bias would rank countries differently. In 2004 the Labor and Worklife Program of the Harvard Law School conducted the first Global Labor Survey (GLS) over the Internet.[4] It asked labor specialists around the world to assess the workplace institutions and practices in their country on a seven-point scale, giving a 7 to a country when it was most favorable to labor and a 1 to a country when it was most favorable to business. The bulk of GLS respondents were union activists who view institutional intervention and union power as positive features of an economy in contrast to the Fraser Institute perspective. The ranking of countries on the GLS was in fact negatively correlated with the ranking of countries on the Fraser Institute scales, as we would expect given the reverse-coding of what is high and what is low. Among the eighteen high-income countries for which the survey obtained responses, the United States ranked at the bottom of the Global Labor Survey on favorable ratings of labor practices on issue after issue: freedom of association and collective bargaining, labor disputes, employee benefits, employment regulations, and working conditions.[5] There is no left-

Figure 1.2   Countries Rated by OECD Measures of Percentage
of Workers Covered by Collective Bargaining and
Government Social Spending

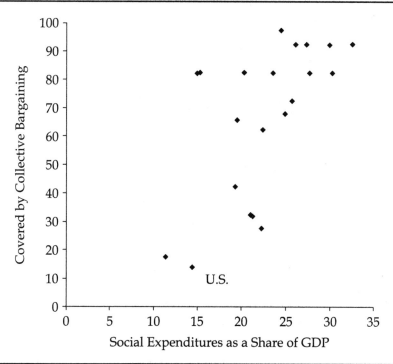

Source: OECD, *Employment Outlook 2004*, ch. 3; social expenditures from
OECD.
Note: The higher the value, the more institution-oriented the country is.

right disagreement about the exceptional reliance of the United
States on markets rather than institutions to determine outcomes.

Finally, moving away from composite indicators and views of
experts, figure 1.2 displays measures of actual wage-setting procedures and government expenditures for the social well-being of citizens from a third source, the Organization of Economic Cooperation and Development (OECD), the international think tank for
advanced market countries. The vertical axis of the figure gives the
percentage of workers whose wages are set by collective bargaining

11

between employers and unions. While unions and firms pay attention to market realities in their bargaining, they produce different settlements than the "invisible hand"—or, more properly, than market forces operating through the visible hand of management. The data show that the percentage of workers whose wages are set by collective bargaining varies considerably across countries, from nearly the entire workforce in several European countries to 30 to 40 percent in Canada, the United Kingdom, New Zealand, and Japan, down to 14 percent in the United States around 2000. Japan is the only country with a lower share of social expenditures than the United States.

The near-universal reliance on collective bargaining in many European Union countries is not simply the result of greater unionization of their workforces. The Scandinavian countries have 70 to 90 percent of their workers in unions, but many other European countries have no more than 30 percent of their workers in unions. France has a smaller proportion of workers in unions than does the United States; around 8 percent of French workers are union members, but in France collective bargaining sets nearly everyone's wages.[6] The reason is that France and several other countries extend the collective bargaining agreements negotiated by the unions and employer federations to all firms and workers in the relevant sector or region. Extension of these settlements outside of the bargaining unit shows the nation's commitment to collective negotiations rather than to the labor market as the mode of wage setting.

The horizontal axis of figure 1.2 displays the share of GDP that each country allocates to public social expenditures. Public social expenditures exclude government spending on defense and interest payments and focus on spending that affects the distribution of economic outcomes among citizens—health care, social security, unemployment insurance, and the like. These data show that, of all the advanced countries, the United States spends the smallest share of GDP for social purposes.[7]

Figure 1.2 is configured so that an economy that relies extensively on the market to set wages and has modest government social expenditures lies near the origin, while an economy that makes extensive use of collective bargaining and government to determine outcomes lies on the upper right-hand side of the figure. Thus, the Nordic countries, with their extensive welfare states, lie at the upper-right part of the figure, and the United States lies at the lower-left part of the figure. Most other advanced countries are closer to the Nordics than to the United States. Even the English-speaking countries—the United Kingdom, Canada, Australia, New Zealand, and Ireland—which are close to the United States in their institutions, lie much further from the free-market point.[8]

Exceptional in Mobility and Job Security

Markets depend on the mobility of workers and firms to adjust to economic problems. Workers who have a problem at their workplace are expected to quit their job rather than try to convince the employer to improve the situation. The country-and-western song "Take This Job and Shove It," which rose high in the charts in the 1970s, reflects this aspect of the American job market. It is hard to imagine any other advanced country with this attitude.

Similarly, on the employer side, firms lay off workers readily. The statement "You're fired," which Donald Trump made famous on the TV show *The Apprentice*, reflects this aspect of the American job market. So too do the stories about employers instructing employees to train low-wage overseas replacements for their jobs prior to offshoring the job and firing the U.S. worker. By contrast, European economies that use institutions to determine labor outcomes rely on *social dialogue* and collective bargaining to make decisions about layoffs rather than allowing firms to act on the basis of management's perception of market forces alone.

Consistent with the market reliance on mobility, workers in the United States are more likely to change employers than those in Europe or Japan. In the United States at any point in time, a typical worker has been at the same employer for 6.7 years, which compares to about 10.6 years for a worker in the EU[9] and fifteen or more years for someone in a large firm in Japan.[10] The typical U.S. worker has many more jobs over his or her working life compared to the typical EU or Japanese worker, in large part because young Americans shop for a good job at the outset of their careers by trying one

13

job, then trying another job, then another, whereas young Europeans and Japanese wait to find a first good job and are more likely to stay with that job for a longer period. The job-to-job mobility rate for Americans is on the order of 3.2 percent per month, or 38 percent per year, compared to a mobility rate among Europeans of just 8.2 percent per year.[11] As a result, U.S. firms are more likely to seek ways to reduce worker quits and turnover, which create recruitment and training expenses, than firms in the European Union or Japan, which are more interested in moving older workers to retirement or to disability insurance.

Americans are also more mobile geographically than persons in other advanced countries. The idea of moving from the East Coast to the West Coast, from Connecticut to Texas (as the Bush clan did), or from Mississippi to New York does not raise an eyebrow. Horace Greeley said, "Go west, young man," not because the Beach Boys told him California girls were the best or because the climate beat the winter winds off the Great Lakes, but because the West was where economic opportunity and jobs were growing most rapidly. In the United States, the odd person out is the one who stays in the same state or city for an entire lifetime when economic opportunities shift geographically.

Europe and Japan are quite different. Capital cities always attract migrants from elsewhere in a country, but many people remain in the city or area where they were born and raised. Every year 7.2 percent of EU citizens change their place of residence compared to 16.2 percent of U.S. citizens. The OECD estimates that 4.1 percent of Americans age fifteen to sixty-four migrated across state lines in 2003 compared to an average of 1.1 percent for similarly aged persons in advanced European countries. Net migration flows—which represent shifts in population across areas rather than potentially offsetting gross flows (you move from Louisiana to Illinois and your friend moves from Illinois to Louisiana)—across U.S. states are 0.4 percent per year compared to an average internal net migration within EU countries of 0.18 percent and 0.06 percent in Japan.[12]

The United States also evinces greater movement between unemployment and employment than happens in most other advanced countries. In 2002 about 33 percent of unemployed Americans left that condition in the succeeding month; in Germany, by contrast, the rate of leaving unemployment was about one-sixth as large: just 5 percent of Germany's unemployed left unemployment in the next month.[13] These differences in flows out of unemployment imply large differences in the length of unemployment spells. In the United States, most unemployment spells are three to four months, whereas in Europe many people are unemployed for two to three years. In 2005 the proportion of the German workforce unemployed for more than one year was 5.1 percent, which was the same as the proportion of the workforce unemployed for any length of time in the United States.[14]

One reason Americans are unemployed for shorter periods than Europeans is that Americans cannot afford to be without work for long. Unemployment insurance in the United States typically lasts six months (though the government often extends it in major recessions), whereas unemployment benefits in Europe last for over a year. When unemployed persons use up their benefits, moreover, Europeans have access to other social programs that protect their living standards, whereas Americans have access to little beyond food stamps. Another difference between the two systems is that in the United States benefits replace less of the average worker's pay than do unemployment benefits systems in other countries. The OECD estimates that the U.S. net replacement rate was 54 percent in 2004 compared to 79 percent in most of continental Europe.[15] But many U.S. workers are ineligible for unemployment insurance or other social programs: fewer than 40 percent of the unemployed received benefits in the late 1990s and early 2000s.[16] As a stark contrast, unemployment benefits in Sweden replace 80 percent of the earnings of the average worker. The result is that unemployed workers must find work quickly in the United States, and they do. With a lower safety net for workers, the United States could not tolerate double-digit rates of joblessness for extended periods, as several European countries have done.

If the United States were to combine a higher rate of exit from unemployment with a lower rate of employed workers going into unemployment, it would always have lower unemployment than other countries. But under the "employment at will" doctrine that governs the U.S. market, firms can eliminate jobs readily. This translates into low job security for U.S. workers and sizable flows of workers from employment to unemployment. In 2002, for example, 1.6 percent of the U.S. working-age population became unemployed in a month, compared to just 0.4 percent of the German working-age population.[17]

One important reason for the lower rate of job loss in Europe is that European countries have employment protection legislation that gives workers some implicit ownership of jobs. Firms negotiate with elected groups of workers in works councils about the conditions for laying workers off or closing plants. This slows the job loss process. In addition, firms have to pay sizable severance pay, which discourages layoffs. In Japan, the system of lifetime employment for workers in the large companies has historically produced only a modest flow of workers from employment to unemployment. But the European and Japanese institutions that reduce job destruction also reduce job creation. A firm that knows it will be costly to lay off workers is less willing to hire workers than one that can do the Donald Trump "you're fired" bit whenever it feels it is necessary. On net, rates of job churning—defined as the rate of creating new jobs and eliminating old jobs—are no higher in the United States than in the EU.[18]

What differs is the churning of workers among jobs. When the difference in the probability of moving from unemployment to employment (higher in the United States) is proportionately greater than the difference in the probability of moving from employment to unemployment (also higher in the United States), unemployment is lower in the United States. This occurred from the 1990s through the mid-2000s. But the relative probabilities of moving from employment to unemployment and vice versus are not fixed. From the 1950s through the 1980s, the difference in the rate of job loss in the United States compared to Europe was proportionately greater than the U.S.-European difference in the rate of job creation. This produced higher unemployment in the United States than in the EU.

Americans are also exceptional in their mobility across firms: they move from one firm to another in pursuit of better employment to a greater extent than workers in other advanced countries. The strongest predictor of whether workers will quit a firm for another job is job satisfaction, which depends on many things: how supervisors treat workers, whether workers get the training they expected, whether they have a union to protect their rights at work, how their skills and preferences match the demands of the job, and their pay relative to that of others. Workers who report a substantial drop in job satisfaction are especially likely to quit and find a new job. They usually report higher job satisfaction on the new job than on the job they left. Indeed, the satisfaction on the new job is similar to the satisfaction they reported before the drop in satisfaction that led them to switch employers. The market worked for them.[19]

But market mobility does not work perfectly. Job applicants are often unaware of the problems at the workplace and thus accept jobs that turn out to be worse than they expected, whereupon they quit. For example, workers who get injured on a job often quit, but since they are gone, they do not warn job applicants or new employees about the risks.[20] The new employee takes the job without full knowledge of the risks involved. The market also does not work well for firms that would like to find out why workers quit their jobs so as to correct the problems. Some employers ask workers through exit interviews why they are quitting, but the person who leaves has little incentive to respond thoughtfully or truthfully.

Exceptional in Labor Regulations

All countries have rules and regulations that protect workers. During the Great Depression, the United States introduced a host of labor protections, from the minimum wage to overtime pay for hours in excess of the standard workweek to procedures for workers to vote on union status and for unions to bargain collectively with employers. From the 1960s through the 1980s, Congress enacted more laws protecting workers from discrimination, insuring private pensions, regulating health and safety, and so on. Although U.S. courts give the federal government preemption over states in areas where Congress has enacted federal laws, states have also passed many

17

laws protecting workers. The notion that the United States is an un-regulated Wild West in the labor area is untrue.

But U.S. labor regulations differ from those of most other advanced countries. The United States (like the other major English-speaking countries) derives its labor regulations and codes from the English common law and legal tradition. Continental European countries follow French or Germanic legal traditions. English legal tradition is more market-oriented and less state-oriented than the others, and the United States fits into that tradition.[21] Thus, while most other countries rely on governmental regulations and decisions or consultations between management and works councils to enforce laws or contracts, the United States relies on the court system. If you face discrimination at your workplace, you can go to the Equal Employment Opportunity Commission (EEOC) or to an equivalent state-level agency, but the final authority rests with the courts. If your employer fires you for union activity, you can go to the National Labor Relations Board (NLRB), but the final authority, again, belongs to the courts.

What American Exceptionalism Means for U.S. Labor Markets

Labor in the United States has differed historically in important ways from European labor. The United States has avoided a great class divide between "workers" and "bourgeoisie." Americans were never particularly attracted to socialism or to the labor or socialist political parties associated with unions. These differences constitute much of the American exceptionalism that has exercised historians and that they attribute in part to the U.S. frontier and the historical scarcity of labor relative to land, which offered many persons the opportunity to be independent farmers and thus contributed to American individualism.[22] But U.S. labor history also has a darker side, including slavery until the Civil War and discrimination against blacks thereafter, as well as violent repression of worker efforts to form unions and then more subtle anti-union activity thereafter. The mass immigration to the United States of persons from different parts of Europe during the nineteenth century and the early decades of the twentieth century further differentiated the United States from Europe. The result has been distinct ways of operating that make the United States the "exceptional labor market" of this book's title.[23]

How does the exceptional nature of the U.S. labor market affect the efficiency of the market and the economy more broadly? In the invisible hand model, supply and demand interact to clear markets efficiently. In this model, there is no space for institutions and regulations to improve the functioning of the market. They may help society obtain other goals, but always at the cost of efficiency. The question then becomes, how close does the U.S. labor market come to being the ideal market model? Some economists, mostly with a conservative bent, believe that the U.S. labor market comes very close. Other economists, mostly with a leftish bent, believe that the real market is far from perfect. The policy debate among advanced countries that pits the U.S. brand of capitalism against the European Union form, the Japanese model, and other variants—the so-called War of the Models[24]—revolves around who is right. To get an answer we must look at how the U.S. labor market actually works. That is the subject of the next six chapters.

∽ CHAPTER 2 ∽

WHEN MARKETS DRIVE OUTCOMES

May the Invisible Hand be with you.

At the turn of the twenty-first century, the U.S. labor market did better in two important ways than the labor market of most other advanced countries. The United States generated rising employment relative to the working-age population while European Union countries were mired in low employment and lengthy spells of high unemployment rates. The United States also generated large gains in productivity as it moved into a more knowledge-based "new economy." The combination of rising employment per adult and increased productivity brought about a substantial growth in GDP per capita that could have improved the living standards of all U.S. citizens and enabled the United States to maintain its economic edge in output per capita over other advanced countries. Huzzah for the market-driven labor market.

But the United States also experienced one great failure in the labor market. It failed to distribute the gains from economic growth and rising productivity to workers in the form of rising real wages and benefits. Looking at the flat or declining growth of real wages for the average American worker, most observers would think that the economy had stagnated. Family incomes rose modestly, but this was because more households had two earners rather than because the earnings of workers rose. In the 2000s, reductions in employer-paid pensions and increased employee premiums for health insurance cut into the economic well-being of even two-earner families. Market-driven labor market? Boo, hiss!

This chapter describes the successes and failures of the U.S. labor market. It asks why real wages did not increase with productivity, as they had in past decades. Stagnant real wages when productivity grows at a healthy clip is not what a market-driven labor system is supposed to deliver. As Einstein might have said, the "invisible hand" may be subtle, but it is not malicious. Could it be that the most market-driven labor system falls spectacularly short of the competitive ideal?

Success in Employment: The Great Jobs Machine

Jobs, jobs, jobs. Who wants a job?

During much of the post–World War II period, Western Europe and Japan generated rising employment and lower unemployment rates than the United States. One of my Australian friends used to say to me, "We teach competitive labor market theory, but we don't believe it. In Australia, judges on a commission set wages after hearing management and labor lawyers argue for lower or higher wages, and we have 1 percent unemployment. Compare that to the U.S. The market determines wages, and unemployment exceeds 5 percent. Only a nutter would believe that the market theory was right. It's a good story for the textbooks, but . . ."

This attitude, common also in Western Europe throughout much of the post–World War II period, came to an end in the decades of the 1990s and 2000s, when unemployment in other advanced countries rose above U.S. unemployment. Figure 2.1 compares unemployment rates, employment per adult, and hours worked per adult between the United States and advanced Europe in 1970 and 2005. In 1970 the United States had a higher unemployment rate than Europe and a lower employment-to-population rate. American adults worked 2 percent fewer hours than Europeans. But in the ensuing decades, employment per adult and hours worked per adult in the United States increased relative to employment and hours in other advanced countries. In 2005 Americans worked 15 percent more hours than Europeans and 27 percent more than the traditionally hardworking Germans.[1] For the first time in modern economic history, the United States had lower unemployment than most EU countries. This reversal of historic patterns led many Eu-

21

Figure 2.1   Unemployment Rates, Employment per Adult, and
Hours Worked per Adult, the United States and
Advanced Europe, 1970 and 2005

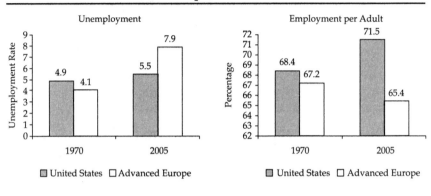

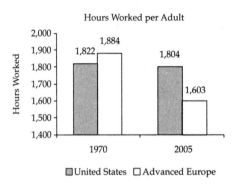

Source: OECD, EU-15 for advanced Europe; hours data are from 2005, *OECD Employment Outlook* 2006, table F 1970, weighted by employment 1970. *OECD Employment Outlook* 1989, table I, which is based on six countries for which data exist—France, Italy, Norway Sweden, Finland, and Germany. The trend in hours from 1970 through 2005 is similar if 2005 refers solely to those countries. For charts of OECD hours, see Evans, Lippoldt, and Marianna (2001) "Trends in Working Hours in OECD Countries." *OECD Labour Market and Social Policy Occasional Papers,* no. 45.

ropean analysts and policymakers to view the United States as the peak capitalist economy—an exemplar of market-driven success whose mode of operation they should mimic. Many American economists also extolled the U.S. system as the only successful way to organize a capitalist economy. As for Australia, it abandoned most of its system of using legal awards to set minimum wages in favor of a more market-driven system.

Why did the United States change from being the high-unemployment economy of advanced capitalism to a low-unemployment economy? Examining the trend in unemployment in the United States shows that the answer has little to do with the United States and a lot to do with the other advanced countries. The average rate of unemployment in the United States, decade by decade, has been: 1950s, 4.5; 1960s, 4.8; 1970s, 6.2; 1980s, 7.3; 1990s, 5.8; 2000s, 5.2.[2] The low rate of the 1950s and 1960s rose in the 1970s with the oil shock, rose again in the 1980s, then fell in the 1990s and 2000s, but to levels that still exceeded those in the 1950s and 1960s. The better performance of the United States relative to Europe was due to the generation in Europe of higher unemployment from the 1980s through the 2000s than in the 1950s and 1960s, not to lower unemployment rates in the United States than in the past. Even traditionally full-employment Sweden had an economic crisis that created high unemployment in 1991, and it failed to return to its previous low rate of unemployment through the mid-2000s.

Many economists have tried to understand what went wrong in Europe. In the early 1990s, the OECD blamed Europe's poor employment record on rigidities in European labor markets—employment protection legislation, collective bargaining, and the like. But as analysts looked more carefully at the evidence, they backed off from this story. The links between labor institutions and outcomes were too weak or unstable to provide a strong case against labor institutions. German unemployment deteriorated relative to American unemployment without any change in German or U.S. labor institutions. It is not easy to explain changes in outcomes by institutions when the institutions have not changed. Some analysts have shifted from blaming EU labor markets for EU joblessness to blaming EU product market rigidities, such as the greater difficulty in opening and closing businesses in many European countries compared to the United States. Others blame high taxes in Europe. But again, European product market institutions and tax policies have not changed markedly over time.

A subtler story is that market-driven economies do better than institution-driven systems in periods of great economic flux because markets are more flexible than institutions. This fits some of the evidence. The 1990s through the 2000s was a period of major economic change: the Soviet empire collapsed, Germany was reunified, and China and India joined the global economic system. But some small advanced European economies maintained low unemployment in the period, and Canada, whose labor institutions resemble those in the United States, had a disastrous economic performance in the 1990s. Moreover, the economic world had also been in flux in the 1950s and 1960s as the world economy recovered from World War II. It is hard to see why European labor markets behaved so differently in the recessions and recoveries at the turn of the twenty-first century than in the earlier decades. Perhaps the low rates of unemployment in the early postwar period were the aberration—the result of huge demand for labor to rebuild destroyed economies. Perhaps U.S. monetary policy under Federal Reserve chief Alan Greenspan was better in dealing with economic problems in the 1990s than the policies of the European Central Bank. My suspicion is that the German economic policies associated with the reunification of East Germany with West Germany placed an intolerable economic burden on Western Europe.

Presumably for political reasons, West Germany gave a one-for-one exchange rate between the East German and West German marks and provided generous social benefits for East Germans, at the cost of high taxes. In addition, West German unions bargained for the same wages and benefits in the East as they gained for workers in the West, as if East Germany was as productive as West Germany. They did this in part to protect West German workers from low-wage Eastern competition and in part in the hope that government subsidies of investment in the East would rapidly raise productivity there. The high wages in the East did protect West German union members from competition, but at the cost of high East German unemployment and taxes to cover the social benefits.

There is a clearer story about the underpinnings of the rapid growth of U.S. employment. The success of the "great U.S. jobs machine," as the Europeans call it, is impressive, irrespective of how advanced Europe fared. Running for president in 1992, candidate Bill Clinton promised millions more jobs if he was elected. It sounded like campaign balderdash when he made the promise, but after recovering slowly from the 1990 recession, employment grew steadily through 2000 so that there were 18.4 million more persons employed after Clinton than before Clinton.[3] Employment grew so rapidly that the ratio of employment to the working-age population rose to a historic peak. Indeed, the late 1990s expansion of the economy led some analysts to believe that the United States had abolished the business cycle. The "new economy" was supposedly on a path of perpetual full-employment growth. Uncork the champagne bottles. Invest in a dot-com and grow rich.

But like previous cyclic booms, the dot-com bubble came to an end with a huge stock market crash. The ensuing recession was modest, however, and even in the "jobless recovery" that followed, unemployment remained low and the rate of employment to population higher than in any period in U.S. history save for the late 1990s. The great jobs machine slowed down, but it did not crash.

Jobs, jobs, jobs—who wants a job? What underlies the success of the United States in creating jobs compared to other advanced countries? Two economic agents have been particularly important: women and immigrants.

Cherchez la Femme . . . l'Ouvrière

In many ways the great success of the U.S. labor market has been in amalgamating millions of women into full-time careers. The facts are these. In 1970, 43.3 percent of U.S. women were in the workforce. In 2005, 59.3 percent were in the workforce.[4] Roughly half of the growth of employment from 1990 to 2005 was in the employment of women. Despite the increased number of working women, the wages of women rose relative to men, and women moved into higher-paying, more-skilled occupations. American women worked more hours than women in Europe and Japan while also having more children than women in those countries. American women averaged 28.7 hours per week in the market, whereas European women averaged 20.7 hours per week. Supermom, how do you do it?

U.S. women do it by reducing the time they spend in traditional household production—food preparation, child care, elderly care, housecleaning. In a typical week, U.S. women now spend ten hours per week less in household work than European women.[5] They spend three hours less per week cooking meals and also spend less time taking care of relatives and doing all of the other activities involved in household production. Those with children under three years of age spend seven hours per week less on child care than their European peers.

So how do U.S. families get these traditional household activities done? Americans eat enough to lead the world in obesity. American homes, which are larger than European homes, are clean, though perhaps not Swiss-level spic and span. The elderly receive care. And American three-year-olds do not wander the streets like lost puppies. One possibility is that American men have increased their household work by enough to replace the time that women are now devoting to work. This, however, is not the explanation. American men are also working long hours and have increased their household work time only modestly. What American households have done is to *marketize* household activity. They use cleaning services to clean their homes. They buy meals in restaurants or as takeout. They send their children to day care.

The evidence on eating is illustrative. Americans spend twice as much on restaurant meals per capita as do Europeans, and as a result, the United States employs approximately twice as many persons per capita in the restaurant and hotel business (which the national accounts data group as a single sector) as European countries such as France. More restaurants than France? Sacre bleu! One of my French economist friends found this disturbing. Think of all the charming cafés and bistros and Michelin star restaurants en Paris. Could Cleveland, Ohio, or Des Moines, Iowa, compete with Paris or Lille or even a small French village in culinary excellence? Perhaps not, but for takeout fast food, the United States has France and every other country beat by a mile. Per capita, the United States has more McDonald's restaurants . . . and more Burger Kings . . . and more Chinese takeouts . . . and more Mexican taco stands . . . than any other country. We trail Britain in curry takeouts, but as more Indians and Pakistanis and Bangladeshis immigrate to the United States, we will catch up quickly.

The most demanding household task is raising children, and here too Americans rely more on the market than do people in most other countries. Americans are twice as likely to use formal day care arrangements as Europeans. The United States has an extensive system of nurseries and after-school programs. Those who can afford to hire a nanny often do. Some firms even have nurseries at their worksite so that their employees with young children can more readily devote hours and effort to work. Those who cannot pay for formal child care make arrangements with neighbors and relatives to take care of their children while they work. Without a vibrant market in child care, U.S. women would never have been able to commit themselves to work as they have. In every country, a greater provision or lower cost of formal child care arrangements is strongly associated with greater time worked by mothers.[6]

So, are U.S. women the overworked females of the Western world? If we add time spent in household work to time spent in market work to obtain total time worked, the answer is no. U.S. women do not work more than European women. The amount of time worked in the home and in the market is roughly the same.[7] U.S. women substitute work in the market for work in the household at almost a one-to-one rate. As computers and the Internet increase the potential for working at home, I expect women and to a lesser extent men to combine the two forms of work more in the future. Already a substantial number of Americans take advantage of modern communication technology to work out of their home rather than at a worksite. In 2005, 20.7 million persons, or 15 percent of non-agricultural workers in the United States, reported working at home at least once a week. Eighty-one percent reported using a computer, and 70 percent reported using the Internet for this work.[8] Multitasking at home makes it harder to differentiate time worked in the market from time spent in household production.

Marketization of household production activities has a dual impact on the employment of women.[9] On the one side, it gives many women time to work in the labor market. Since many U.S. women are highly educated—35 percent more women than men graduated from colleges and universities in 2003[10]—the marketization of household production gives the U.S. economy a huge skilled workforce that it would not otherwise have. On the other side, there is a knock-on effect of marketization of household activities on the employment of other workers. The purchase of meals, cleaning services, and child care services raises demand for labor in these sectors. Some of this work—for instance, in restaurants or cleaning—is low-paid and done by less-educated persons, often immigrants. Some of the work, such as child care, is performed by more-educated persons (often at lower wages than they could get in other jobs) who take care of enough children to make it economical for families to buy the service.

The economic calculus facing a woman and her family is whether she can make sufficiently high earnings, net of taxes, to pay for market services and raise family income. The lower the tax rate, the higher her wages, and the lower the cost of household goods and services, the more likely it is that the woman will choose to work. American college graduate women generally can earn enough in the market to make the decision between doing household work and market work a no-brainer.[11]

In short, the market-driven United States creates more employment than Europe through exceptional marketization of household activity. This is more important than differences in collective bargaining, employment protection legislation, or many other labor market institutions that garner more attention.

How has the United States managed to be exceptional in marketizing household work? Several factors appear to play a role: the tax breaks given to child care; the responsiveness of school systems to the desire of parents for after-school programs; the high return to education and inequality in earnings, which makes it financially sensible for women in professional and managerial jobs to work full-time and to buy meals, cleaning, and child care from lower-paid workers; and the availability of an ample supply of low-paid immigrants who can provide these services.

Immigrants

Give me your poor, your huddled masses—er, your best scientists and smartest students, your star athletes . . .

The second reason for U.S. employment success is that the number of immigrants coming to the country increased greatly at the end of the twentieth century. Immigrants made up approximately half of the 1990s job growth in the United States. During the slower job growth from 2000 to 2005, when native-born employment was roughly constant, immigration added over two million new workers.[12] The large increase in immigration began when Congress enacted the 1965 Immigration Act, which ended quotas based on national origin. In the 1960s, the other immigrant-receiving English-speaking countries, Canada, Australia, and New Zealand, admitted more immigrants than the United States. But by the 2000s, the United States admitted over twice as many immigrants as those countries combined and experienced significant illegal immigration as well, which made the United States the single largest recipient of immigrants in the world by far. In 2000 the 35 million immigrants to the United States constituted 12.4 percent of the population, up from 4.7 percent in 1970. Because most immigrants are of working age, they make up nearly one in five persons age twenty-five to thirty-nine years old.[13]

Immigrants tend to be either relatively unskilled or highly skilled. The millions of immigrants from Mexico and Latin America often have little education. They come, many illegally, for a better life in the United States than is possible in their economically deprived homelands. Immigrants from Europe and Asia tend to be more skilled. Although India is one of the poorest countries in the world, Indian immigrants to the United States are almost all college graduates, many with expertise in engineering and computer sciences. The greater the distance a country is from the United States, the more likely it is that its immigrants will be highly skilled. Peasants from Asia cannot cross a land border to find work in the United States. Peasants from Mexico can.

During the 1990s boom, demand for science and engineering specialists increased greatly in the United States. Business, universities, and the government managed to hire large numbers of new specialists in these fields without generating shortages or driving up their wages relative to wages in other fields. The United States did this by importing scientists and engineers from overseas. Many international students obtained green cards and stayed to work in the United States after earning their degrees. For example, a 2003 study showed that 92 percent of Chinese doctorates were still working in the country seven years after gaining a PhD in the United States.[14] Many scientists and engineers educated overseas also migrated to the United States. Nearly 60 percent of the *growth* in the number of U.S.-based PhD scientists and engineers from 1990 to 2000 came from the foreign-born. Forty percent of the growth in the number of scientists and engineers with a bachelor's degree also came from the increased numbers of foreign-born persons in scientific and engineering occupations.[15]

The contribution of highly educated immigrants to U.S. scientific and technological prowess is easy to see. Go into any university lab in the United States and you will find international students. Sixty percent of the postdocs, who do hands-on laboratory research in biological and medical sciences, come from overseas. In 2000 over half of PhD natural scientists age forty-five or younger were born outside the United States.[16] Several years ago I asked participants at a conference organized by GREAT (Group on Graduate Research, Education, and Training), the association of research-oriented medical schools, to imagine how their hospitals, labs, and classrooms would operate if, through some disaster, the foreign-born went home. Faces went blank. Lab benches would be empty, as would podiums in classrooms. In some cases, the classrooms themselves would be nearly empty. Many conference participants would have disappeared as well.

Immigrants affect employment in the United States in ways that go beyond simply adding to the supply of labor. Some immigrants create employment opportunities for native residents. Immigrant scientists and engineers help advance the knowledge that keeps American firms in leading positions in the world. Immigrant medical researchers contribute to the medical advances that produce healthier working lives. Immigrant professors teach students the skills that make them more productive. Immigrant entrepreneurs help form businesses like Google and Intel. They almost certainly set up your local Chinese or Mexican restaurant. Less-skilled immigrants provide many of the day care and restaurant and cleaning services that enable U.S. women to enter the job market full-time by freeing them from household tasks.

This does not mean that immigration is entirely a positive on the nation's economic balance sheet. Immigration benefits a country's economy in part by lowering the wages or harming the job prospects of residents with skills similar to immigrants' skills. When immigrants take jobs that Americans do not want and would not take even with higher wages (but not so high that no one would buy the products), immigrants benefit everyone in the country. But the number of such jobs is limited. Most immigrants compete with Americans for jobs and thus reduce the earnings and employment opportunities for U.S. citizens and residents in those occupations in which they are competing. Indeed, the reduction in the wages of those workers or of the costs of the goods and services constitutes the benefit of immigration to the rest of the society. For example, the immigration of doctors benefits Americans without an "MD" after their name because it increases the supply of medical services. Let more foreign doctors into the country and the availability of medical care will rise and its price will fall. Let enough foreign doctors into the country and maybe doctors will make house visits as they did half a century ago! But U.S. doctors lose from foreign competition. Recognizing this, the American Medical Association (AMA) makes it difficult for foreign-trained doctors to practice in the United States. To take another case, baseball fans benefit from the skills of the 40 percent or so of professional ballplayers who are immigrants. But the immigrants make it harder for the American kid who wants to play professional baseball to make it to the big leagues. Today Joe Hardy would have greater trouble breaking into the lineup of the Washington Senators (now the Nationals) than would have been the case in 1955, when *Damn Yankees* opened on Broadway.[17]

To the extent that immigrants are primarily lower-skilled workers, they add to earnings inequality by reducing the economic position of the lower-paid persons with whom they compete (often earlier groups of immigrants). By contrast, to the extent that immigrants are highly skilled, they reduce earnings inequalities. In fact, the flow of immigrants to the United States tends to be bimodal: great numbers of both low-skill workers and high-skill workers come to the country.

Finally, the biggest beneficiaries of immigration are the immigrants themselves, particularly those from lower-income countries where earnings are far below American earnings. The chance to earn four to six times as much in the United States as in their native countries induces millions of less-educated Mexicans and Central Americans to enter the country in any way they can. Demographers estimate that seven million illegal immigrants were working in the country in 2005. Given the huge economic incentives to work in the United States and the long border with Mexico, about one-tenth of employed Mexicans were working in the United States in the early 2000s—four times as many as were legally admitted.[18] The market forces driving this flow of less-skilled labor are powerful: the immigrant benefits from higher wages, the U.S. employer profits from labor willing to work for less than Americans, and consumers benefit from lower-priced goods and services. If the country decides to reform the immigration system and reduce the illegal flows, it will be no easy task. Fighting market forces is not natural in a market-driven labor system.

Success in Productivity

Productivity growth is the penicillin for most economic illnesses—the magic bullet that allows economies to produce more with less. In a competitive economy, higher productivity translates into lower prices and better living standards for all. It does not matter if the growth in productivity comes from workers investing in skills or from firms investing in machinery or software or from increases in the stock of useful knowledge due to R&D or the bright ideas of some inventor. It also does not matter if workers take the benefits of higher productivity in additional output (a bigger house or more cars, as many Americans prefer) or in fewer hours worked (extra vacation or holiday time, as many Europeans prefer), or in some combination thereof. Higher productivity in a competitive economy should translate into higher real wages.

For a century or so, productivity and the real wages of regular workers increased together. Productivity increased because Americans invested in public education so that skills improved and because workers shifted from low-productivity agriculture and less-skilled manufacturing to higher-value-added manufacturing and later to knowledge-intensive professional and white-collar work. During the great "automation scare" in the early 1960s, when some feared that automated factories would bring back the mass unemployment of the Great Depression, almost all economists argued that automation-induced productivity gains would raise real wages and benefit workers, as productivity gains had done historically.[19]

Why were economists so sure that automation was good when the world had not seen automated factories, robotics, and other potential worker-eliminating technologies? What about the workers displaced by the new technology? The logic of productivity growth in a competitive economy is that increased productivity allows for economic expansion that creates new jobs for displaced workers. If consumers are sufficiently enamored of the new or improved products or lower prices that automation produces or permits, they may buy enough of those goods to increase employment in the sectors with rapid productivity rise. But if not, so what? Higher productivity increases living standards and thus the income to purchase other goods and services. As long as monetary and fiscal policy are sensible, the competitive system guarantees that productivity due to automation or anything else will benefit labor. The workers will find jobs elsewhere in the economy, although not necessarily in the same activities or at the same pay.[20]

In the 1970s and 1980s, when firms began introducing computers into the productive process, economists and businesspeople expected productivity to rise. For a while, however, there was no apparent productivity dividend. Robert Solow famously remarked, "We see computers everywhere but in the productivity statistics."[21] The Solow paradox disappeared in the 1990s when productivity growth in the United States zoomed. It rose in manufacturing. It rose in services. It rose more rapidly than in the past and more rapidly than in most other advanced countries. And it rose most of all in industries that had made greater investments in computer technologies. As best we can tell, the delay between computerization and productivity growth occurred because firms and workers needed time to learn how to use the new all-purpose technological advance most effectively.

But the rise in productivity created a new paradox: the failure of real wages to grow. Instead of the Solow paradox, we have the real wage paradox—productivity everywhere but in the real wage statistics. In Moscow in 1984, I was troubled about the sluggish growth of real wages, but at that time the break between productivity growth and real wage growth was too recent to have gained the attention of many economists. The oil price shocks of the 1970s had created inflation, fuel shortages, and joblessness as economies worldwide adjusted to the increased share of global output going to the oil-producing nations. The Nixon administration was so concerned about the danger of a wage-price explosion that it introduced price and wage controls from 1974 to 1976—the last thing one would have expected from a Republican, business-oriented administration. Many believed that once the economy had adjusted to the shock, real wages would regain their historic link to productivity growth.

The Failure of Real Wages to Grow

As figure 2.2 shows, this did not happen. The measure of earnings that allows for the longest historical comparisons is the average hourly earnings of production and nonsupervisory workers in private industry. These workers made up 81 percent of the U.S. private

34

Figure 2.2   Growth of Productivity Compared to Growth of
              Alternative Measures of Real Hourly Earnings, 1959
              to 2005 (1973 = 1.00)

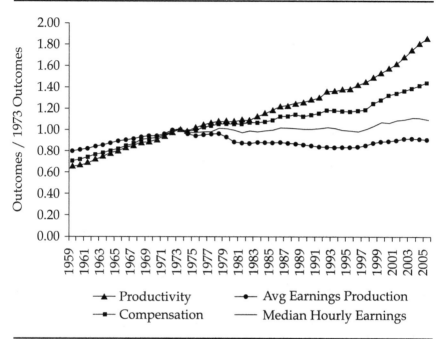

—▲— Productivity   —●— Avg Earnings Production
—■— Compensation   ——— Median Hourly Earnings

Source: Average hourly earnings, production and supervisory workers: *Economic Report of the President* 2006, table, B-47. Productivity, real hourly compensation: *Economic Report of the President* 2006, table B-49 with 2005 updated from http://frwebgate2.access.gpo.gov/cgibin/waisgate.cgi? WAISdocID=971353361824+9+0+0&WAISaction=retrieve. Median hourly earnings: Economic Policy Institute available at http://www.epi.org/ datazone/06/wagecuts_all.xls.

non-agricultural work force in 2005.[22] The Bureau of Labor Statistics (BLS) obtains their nominal earnings by surveying firms and transforms nominal earnings into real earnings by dividing by the consumer price index (CPI). This measure of pay, which had always tracked productivity closely, declined from the 1970s through the early 1990s, and despite some modest increase in the ensuing boom, it remains far below its early 1970s level as of this writing. *Mean* real hourly earnings for production and nonsupervisory workers were 8 percent lower in 2005 than in 1973, even while national output per worker was 55 percent higher in 2005 than in 1973.[23]

Real hourly earnings for much of the workforce were 8 percent lower while productivity was 55 percent higher? If in 1973 any economist had predicted such a pattern, the American Economic Association would have carted him or her off as mad. If someone were to predict that thirty years from now, when productivity is likely to be 55 percent or so higher than today, real earnings will be lower than today, most economists would view that person as mad, even though such a prediction would replicate the past thirty or so years' experience. Productivity and real wages rise together in a market economy.

So what is going on? One possibility is that there is a problem with the production and nonsupervisory workers' earnings series. It excludes white-collar nonproduction workers such as professionals and managers, whose wages rose more rapidly than those of production workers. If we include all workers in the wage series, wages rise more robustly. The Current Population Survey (CPS) provides the most widely used series of earnings for all workers, blue-collar as well as white-collar, in the form of *median* usual weekly earnings. The median is the earnings level that splits the distribution into two equal halves—half make more than the median and half make less. Mean earnings have increased more than median earnings in the United States, so using the median measure could widen the difference in growth between productivity and earnings. But figure 2.2 shows that the growth of the median earnings of all workers is closer to the growth of productivity than the growth of mean earnings for production and nonsupervisory workers. The reason is that the pay of white-collar supervisory and nonproduction workers increased more rapidly than that of the production and nonsupervisory workers covered in the mean hourly earnings series. Still, figure 2.2 shows that the growth of productivity far exceeds the growth of real median earnings for all workers. By this measure, real earnings were 6 percent lower in 2004 than in 1973, compared to the 55 percent growth of productivity.[24]

What else could be going on? One other problem is that hourly or weekly earnings do not measure the full compensation that goes to labor. Earnings data exclude firm-provided health insurance, pensions, and other so-called fringe benefits, which have come to be a larger share of pay over time. We must add those expenditures into the mix. From surveys of firms, the Bureau of Labor Statistics provides estimates of labor compensation that include these expenditures. As can be seen in figure 2.2, these data show greater rises in real compensation than in direct pay, but even here the divergence between productivity growth and growth of real compensation is huge. The puzzle remains.

Did real wage growth fall massively short of productivity growth in other advanced countries whose labor markets are more institutionally driven than the U.S. market? No. Real earnings in virtually all other advanced countries increased substantially, at roughly the same rate as the increase in productivity.[25] Had U.S. earnings risen with productivity as did earnings in those countries, American workers would be making on the order of 60 to 70 percent more than they made. Hourly earnings for production workers in industry in 2005 would have been around $25 instead of $16. That institutionally driven wage systems tie productivity growth and wages together more tightly than in the market-driven United States deepens the puzzle. Could it be that the most market-driven labor market falls short of the invisible hand model in ways that institutions might correct? Where has the increased output in the economy gone?

Who Took the Cookie from the Cookie Jar?

The share of national income that goes to labor equals the compensation paid to workers multiplied by the number of workers divided by the goods and services that workers produce multiplied by the price of those goods and services. If the share of labor in national income is constant, then the growth of real compensation *must* equal the growth of labor productivity. No ifs, buts, or maybes. It is a matter of algebra. Conversely, if real compensation grows less than productivity, labor's share of national income *must* fall. No ifs, buts, or maybes. While U.S. national income statistics show some decline in labor's share of national income, there is no huge downward trend consistent with the fall and stagnation of real earnings shown in the earnings series. Labor received 57.5 percent of national income in 1960, 59.3 percent in 1970, and 56.5 percent in 1980, but then fell to its lowest share on record in 2005, 52.3 percent. Taking all of labor compensation, however, including supplements for pensions, health insurance, and government social insurance, produces a smaller drop in the share of national income going to labor, from 67.7 percent in 1980 to 65.0 percent in 2005.[26] While newspapers linked the declining share of labor with the gap between the growth of productivity and the growth of real wages,[27] changes in labor's share explain only part of the productivity–real wage puzzle. Something else is evidently going on. What is it?

Clues to the resolution of the puzzle can be found in the debates over tax cuts in the United States and in how the government measures earnings and prices.

First, the tax cut clue. When the Bush administration argued for tax cuts to enrich the super-rich, administration economists pointed out that persons with high incomes pay a large and increasing share of the taxes; this argument dates back to the Reagan tax cuts.[28] I was surprised at the numbers they cited. The United States has a progressive tax system that is designed to take a larger share of taxes from rich Americans than from middle- and lower-income Americans. The system is not as progressive as it first appears because the rich have enough money to hire tax specialists to find ways to shield their income from taxes and enough influence on Congress to create numerous tax loopholes.[29] But the basic message had an element of truth. The rich were paying a large and increasing share of taxes because they had a large and increasing share of the country's national income, while the earnings of other Americans had stagnated. The implication is staggering: *most of the productivity growth of the past twenty to thirty years ended up in the pockets of a small number of super-rich Americans.* A claim like this sounds like the kind of extreme propaganda that the Soviet Communists might have made at the 1984 Moscow economic meetings that I described in the introduction. It is an extreme claim. But it is not propaganda. It is the truth. As I lay it out in chapter 3, inequality in earnings in the United States increased so massively over a quarter-century or so of economic growth that the main beneficiaries were a small number of super-rich individuals and families.

The data are clear on this. In the CPS survey, the top 10 percent of earners are the only group whose earnings grew at a pace comparable to the growth of productivity. But the CPS earnings survey understates the increase in earnings for persons with high earnings. It top-codes high earnings so that persons making more than the top-coded value ($150,000 per year in 2005) are reported as earning the top amount rather than what they actually earned.[30] Thus, those who earned more than $150,000, whether $1 million or $10 million, are classified simply as earning more than $150,000 rather than as earning the actual amount they earned. Government statisticians do this so that it is not possible to discover the earnings of particular people from the data. In addition, the earnings statistics do not include the stock options that are a major part of compensation for top executives.

To obtain a better measure of how much earnings have risen for the super-rich, economists examine the tax files of the Internal Revenue Service. These data show huge gains in real earnings for the upper 1 percent and even larger gains for the upper one-tenth of 1 percent. For instance, from 1972 to 2001, when real earnings fell by 0.4 percent for the worker at the middle of the wage and salary distribution, real earnings rose by 34 percent for workers in the upper 10 percent of wage and salary earners. But within the upper 10 percent, much of the increase went to the upper 1 percent, whose earnings rose by 94 percent. And within the upper 1 percent, much of the increase went to the upper 0.1 percent, whose earnings rose by 181 percent. And within the upper 0.1 percent, much of the increase went to the upper 0.01 percent, whose earnings rose by a staggering 497 percent! Half of the growth of wage and salary income went to the upper 10 percent, so that they gained 5 times as much as their share of the workforce, but 36 percent went to the upper 1 percent, who gained 36 times their share of the workforce, and 18 percent went to the upper 0.1 percent, who gained 180 times their share of the workforce. But the really big winners, those in the upper .01 percent, earned 7 percent of the growth of real wages and salaries—or 700 times their share of the workforce.[31] Thus, the changes in the income distribution resemble a Russian babushka doll: inside each doll is a wealthier doll that has taken more of the gain in national output, ad infinitum. The number of millionaires and billionaires increased rapidly, and the gap between their earnings and those of the rest of society grew. When *Forbes* magazine named the four hundred richest Americans for 2005, only billionaires were on the list.[32]

The final factor that helps to explain the difference between the growth of productivity and the growth of real earnings is technical—the way government statisticians measure prices. Government statisticians and economists use the consumer price index to calculate real earnings and use a different price index, the GDP deflator, to calculate productivity growth. The consumer price index has risen more rapidly than the GDP deflator, which produces a smaller growth in real wages than in productivity.[33] Taking account of this difference by deflating wages by the GDP deflator and the measurement issues involved in estimating wages, the growth of real compensation for all workers deflated by the GDP deflator must equal the growth of productivity with GDP also deflated by the GDP deflator when labor's share of national income is constant. And of course it does.

But I have not devoted so much of this chapter to the real wage–productivity paradox to demonstrate that the appropriate accounting resolves the paradox. The real wage–productivity paradox is not about accounting. It is about another aspect of America's exceptional labor market: the economics that put so much of the growth of productivity into the pockets of so few. This aspect of the U.S. market-driven labor system—the distribution of national income—is the subject of the next chapter.

✦ CHAPTER 3 ✦

DISTRIBUTION MATTERS

Americans are traditionally less concerned about income distribution than persons in other countries. As long as wages and incomes rise for everyone, why worry that Bill Gates makes more than all the other Bills in the country taken together? Economists generally stress the fact that inequality—differences in earnings between economic activities—are an incentive to workers. High rewards in some occupations or industries signal workers to shift into those occupations or industries. Labor economists further stress that when workers do so, this eventually reduces the initial inequality. If professional wrestlers earn more than curlers, some curlers will put down their curling brooms and learn how to administer flying drop kicks and arm drags. Better yet, perhaps the curlers will form a villainous tag team that uses their brooms to beat down the good guy "faces." The shift in supply from curling to wrestling will raise the pay in curling and reduce the pay in wrestling. Presto, the market will have reduced the inequality in pay between wrestlers and curlers.

In the late 1960s, when returns to undergraduate education were high, many baby boomers invested in a college education. When they graduated, the increased supply drove down the returns. This pattern induced one young economist (me) to write about "overeducated Americans"—the baby boomer graduates whose entry into the market reduced the returns that they had expected when they chose to go to college—and to applaud the market-induced reduction in inequality.[1] The long-run trend of rising real wages for everyone and of falling or stable income inequality suggested that distributional issues belonged on the back burner. In any case, at the level of inequality in the 1960s and 1970s, a policy of taxing the wealthy and distributing the money to the rest of society would not have increased the income of the average worker all that much. If in 1972 the United States had placed a 10 percent surcharge on the incomes of the upper 1 percent of earners and distributed the money to the lower 80 percent, wage incomes in the lower 80 percent would have risen by 2.7 percent.[2] Given that some of the higher tax would probably have lowered the pretax income of the upper 1 percent as they sought ways to avoid the taxation, the economic return to the bulk of the population would have been modest. Economists could tell their lefty friends to forget about distribution and focus on what really mattered for living standards: the rate of economic growth.

The stagnation of real wages from the 1970s to the present despite healthy economic growth invalidates this facile dismissal of distributional issues. If the United States had maintained the inequality it had when I complained about inequality in Moscow in 1984—call it Ronald Reagan inequality—families in the lower 80 percent of the income distribution would have been $4,000 better off than they were in 2004, measured in 2003 dollars.[3] If in 2001 the country had taxed 10 percent of the income of the upper 1 percent and distributed the money to the lower 80 percent of earners, wage incomes in the lower 80 percent would have risen by 8.3 percent— three times more than they would have in 1972.[4] By the 2000s, inequality in the United States more closely resembled inequality in a developing country than in an advanced capitalist economy.

Inequality Big-Time

Analysts with different perspectives use different words to describe inequality. Persons on the left often refer to one form of inequality, the proportion of persons with incomes less than half the median income, as "relative poverty," presumably because the term "poverty" suggests that something should be done to reduce it. When I worked in the late 1990s with the National Policy Association, an organization of business and labor leaders concerned with national economic issues, the business leaders recommended the use of the term "disparity" to refer to income differences because "inequality" had a leftist connotation. Accordingly, I called the small booklet on inequality that I wrote for the association "When Earnings Diverge," and I used the I-word sparingly in the text. My linguistic preference, and that of most labor economists, is yet another term, "dispersion," which has a more scientific connotation in statistics as referring to any of a set of measures of the scatter or spread of numbers around the central tendency of a distribution—measures such as standard deviation, Gini coefficient, interquartile measure, and ratio of percentile values. Whatever term or measure we use, the United States has the greatest difference in income among its citizens in the advanced world.

Figure 3.1 displays two widely used measures of the inequality—or disparity, or dispersion—of income for advanced countries. The vertical axis shows the Gini coefficient, which measures the overall spread of the distribution of income. The Gini can vary from 0, when all persons have the same income, to 1.0, when one person has all the income, but in fact it ranges from around 0.25 to 0.42, with the United States at the top of the list. The horizontal axis gives a different metric: the ratio of the earnings of persons at the ninetieth percentile of the earnings distribution to the earnings of persons at the tenth percentile. It reflects the pay of those at the upper 10 percent point in the distribution of earnings relative to the earnings of persons at the lower 10 percent point in the distribution. Again, the United States is at the top. Other measures of inequality give the same result. If there were a gold medal for inequality, advanced country division, the United States would win hands down.

In fact, inequality is sufficiently higher in the United States than in other advanced countries that despite its having 25 to 35 percent higher income per capita than those countries, persons in the bottom third of the American income distribution are poorer than persons in the bottom third of the income distribution in advanced Europe or Japan. Measured in terms of "purchasing power parity" (that is, in terms that adjust the value of currencies for differences in the prices of consumer goods and services), workers in the bottom

Figure 3.1   Measures of Inequality, Gini Coefficients and 90/10 Differentials, United States Versus Other Advanced Countries

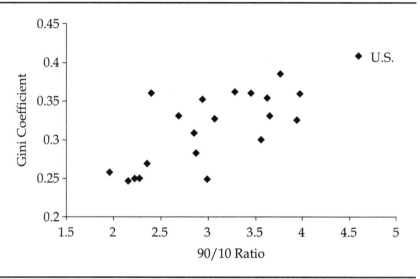

Source: OECD, *Employment Outlook 2004*, table 3.2; United Nations, *Development Report 2005*, table 15.

10 percent of a typical EU country earn about 44 percent more than Americans at the lowest 10 percent of the U.S. distribution.[5] In addition, the European worker has national health insurance and other protections that the American worker buys out of his or her paycheck or does without. Workers at the bottom 10 percent of the German income distribution make about twice as much as workers in the bottom 10 percent of the American income distribution.[6] But there is a flip side to low incomes at the bottom. U.S. billionaires are worth lots more than the wealthiest citizens of other advanced countries! And as Bill Gates and Warren Buffett have proven, at least some U.S. billionaires are generous and responsible with their money.

Finally, standard measures of inequality show that the United States more closely resembles a developing country than an advanced country on this measure of economic performance. The Central Intelligence Agency (CIA) publishes on its website Gini coefficients for most of the countries of the world. In 2006 it gave data for 123 countries for the late 1990s through the mid-2000s. At one end of the inequality spectrum, Denmark has the lowest inequality, with a Gini coefficient of 0.232, while Namibia in Africa has the highest inequality, with a Gini of 0.707. Ranking countries in reverse order of their Gini coefficients, so that countries with less inequality are ranked lower (Denmark is number one), the United States ranks eighty-eighth, which puts it in the bottom third of countries—far below other advanced economies, whose median rank was thirty-fourth. Over half of the developing countries had lower Gini coefficients than the United States.[7]

Why are earnings and income so unequally distributed in the United States?

One possible explanation is that U.S. workers differ more in their skills than do workers in other countries. This explanation does not fly. The primary measure of skills, years of schooling, varies the same or less among workers in the United States than among workers in other advanced countries. The distribution of scores on paper-and-pencil tests of academic skills does vary more in the United States than in many other advanced countries. For instance, on the OECD's international survey of literacy and numeracy, the top fifth of Americans scored 355 compared to a score of 191 for the bottom fifth of Americans—an 86 percent differential—whereas on the same test the top fifth of Swedes scored 367 compared to a score of 243 for the bottom fifth—a 51 percent differential. But schooling has a much stronger relation to earnings than literacy scores. If Americans had the same distribution of years of schooling and the same distribution of literacy on the OECD international literacy survey as other advanced countries, the United States would have just about as much income inequality as shown in figure 3.1.[8]

Another possible explanation for the high level of inequality in the United States is that rewards to skills are larger than in other advanced countries. This is generally true. University graduates earn more relative to high school graduates in the United States than in other advanced countries, and this contributes to the high level of inequality. But this also does not explain much of the difference in inequality between the United States and these other countries. If the differential in earnings between university and high school graduates in the United States dropped to the level in an advanced country with a lower university premium, the United States would still have much greater inequality. Indeed, if the difference in pay between persons with *any* measured characteristics were the same in the United States as in, say, Sweden or Germany or Japan, the United States would still be left with much higher inequality. The reason is that the big difference between the dispersion of earnings in the United States and the dispersion of earnings in other advanced countries occurs among persons with identical measured skills.

Figure 3.2 shows this surprising fact. It compares the dispersion of earnings among Americans with the *same* schooling, age, gender, and scores on the OECD international literacy test with the inequality in earnings among *all* persons in Sweden, the Netherlands, and Germany. The comparison is shocking. Greater inequality in earnings among Americans with the same measured characteristics than among all workers in entire countries? It does not make sense. The competitive market is supposed to produce a single wage for workers with the same set of skills. Perhaps the countries measure income differently. They do a bit, but not enough to matter very much. Perhaps the United States has high inequality because so many U.S. workers are immigrants, whose skills differ from those of natives with the same years of schooling and test scores. This also does not explain the pattern. Inequality is higher among the native-born with similar skills than among all persons in Sweden, the Netherlands, and Germany. No matter how we slice and dice the data, inequality (or disparity or dispersion) of earnings differs massively between the United States and the other advanced countries. Why?

As best I can tell, income inequality is higher in the United States because of America's exceptional reliance on markets to set pay and because of what I call the second law of earnings dispersion: *institutional determination of wages produces less dispersion than does market determination.* (What's the first law? *Heterogeneity among people and jobs creates dispersion in any economic setting.*) Moreover, what is true

Figure 3.2   Earnings Inequality for Americans with Comparable
Literacy Scores Versus Earnings Inequality for All
Workers in Sweden, Germany, and the Netherlands,
Measured by Standard Deviation of Log of Earnings

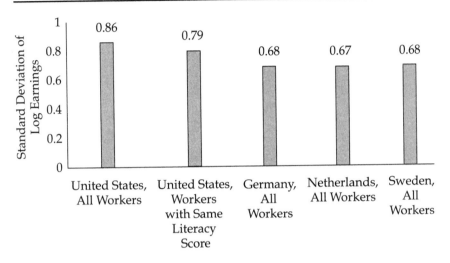

Source: Dan Devroye and Richard Freeman, "Does Inequality in Skills Explain Inequality in Earnings Across Advanced Countries?" working paper 8140 (Cambridge, Mass.: National Bureau of Economic Research, February 2001), figure 3.

across countries is also true within the United States: earnings among unionized workers, whose wages are set by collective bargaining, and the earnings of public-sector workers, whose wages are set by governments or through collective bargaining, are less dispersed than the earnings of otherwise comparable workers in the non-union private sector.

Rising Inequality

When I critiqued the U.S. labor market in Moscow in 1984, I was more troubled by America's increasing income inequality than by the high level of income inequality. In a growing economy, increasing inequality is worse than a high level of inequality. When inequality is stable, even at high levels, economic growth raises the income of persons throughout the income distribution.[9] With stable inequality, the trickle-down view of growth, that what is good for the rich is good for everyone else, has validity, though so too does its mirror image—that what is good for the average person or the poor is good for the rich. By contrast, increased inequality can break the link between economic growth and improved living standards for the bulk of the population, as occurred from the 1970s to the mid-2000s.

Inequality began rising in the United States in the late 1970s and early 1980s and continued increasing through the early 1990s, stabilized or fell slightly in the 1990s boom, and then drifted upward in the 2000s, depending on the measure of income and of inequality.[10] In 1979 the top 10 percent of wage and salary workers earned 3.5 times per hour what the bottom 10 percent earned. In 2005 the top 10 percent earned 5.8 times as much as the bottom 10 percent.[11] Looking at occupations, in 1979 managers earned 1.65 times as much as production workers; in 2005 they earned 2.0 times as much.[12] Looking at educational attainment, in 1979 college graduates earned 1.4 times as much as high school graduates; in 2005 college graduates earned 1.74 times as much as high school graduates.[13] The only lower-paid workers whose wages increased over this period were women, whose pay rose relative to men, though without completely closing the male-female pay gap.

The widening of the income distribution surprised most economists. It reversed the trend toward equalization of income and wealth that the United States had experienced from the World War II period to the early 1970s. During the war periods, the government set up labor boards to minimize industrial disputes and to ensure fairness in pay setting. War labor boards pressured firms to accept unions and favored proportionately higher pay increases to the lower-paid. The reliance on institutions reduced the dispersion of earnings. National policy during those and earlier wars sought to spread the cost of war among the population. The post-9/11 war on terror is the first war in which an administration has made a policy goal of reducing taxes on the rich, which increases inequality and places the burden of the cost of the struggle on ordinary citizens.

In the 1980s the rise in inequality was roughly equally divided between decreases in the income of the lower-paid relative to the median and increases in the income of the higher-paid relative to the median. This polarization of the income distribution generated widespread concern about the decline of the middle class. When the top of the earnings distribution and the bottom of the earnings distribution pull away from the middle, almost any measure of the middle class will show a declining proportion of workers in the middle.

In the 1990s the increase in inequality took a very different form: huge increases in the earnings of persons at the very top of the income distribution compared to everyone else. Between 1987 and 2005, the wages of persons in the upper 5 percent of the wage distribution increased from 2.5 times the median to 2.9 times the median earnings.[14] But the gains of the upper 5 percent were not equally shared. As noted earlier, the upper 1 percent gained relative to the rest, and within the upper 1 percent, it was the upper one-tenth of 1 percent who did really well. It was a great time to be super-wealthy.

Why Did Inequality Increase So Much?

The Clinton administration attributed rising inequality to technological change that shifted demand for labor to higher-paid, skilled workers and away from lower-paid, less-skilled workers. The increased use of computers throughout the economy is our best measure of this technological change. There is some evidence that the new technology favors skilled workers. Earnings are higher for workers who use computers, and the more-educated are more likely to use a computer than the less-educated. Industries that make extensive use of modern technologies tend to have high productivity growth and to employ more highly skilled workers.[15] Other countries, however, also introduced modern computer-driven technologies without increasing inequality as much as the United States did. And as computers have become more widespread—over half the workforce uses them—inequality has not fallen to its good old Ronald Reagan levels.

The decline of unionism contributed to the increase in inequality. Since unions increase the pay of their members, who are primarily in the middle class, and reduce the dispersion of pay among members, the shift from union wage setting to market wage setting added to inequality. I estimate that the decline of unionism accounted for perhaps 20 percent of the rise of inequality, measured as the increase in standard deviation of the log of earnings among all workers.[16] The decline of unionism may have been even more important because managers of non-union firms who once felt that they had to mimic union wage settlements to remain non-union no longer fear organizing drives. However, quantifying this indirect effect is difficult and problematic.

Another institutional force that affects inequality is the minimum wage. The real value of the minimum wage has been tanking since the late 1960s. In 1968 the value of the minimum wage in 2005 dollars was $9.12. Since then, legislated increases in the minimum wage have not kept pace with inflation, so the real value of the minimum wage has trended downward. Between 1997 and 2006, Congress decided against raising the minimum wage from the $5.15 nominal value set for 1997. This is the longest period in U.S. history during which Congress failed to raise the minimum. At $5.15, the minimum is 40 percent lower relative to the price level than it was in 1968. Those working full-time at the minimum make just 55 percent of the 2005 poverty line and thus struggle to pay their rent, heating costs, and food bills. According to the CEO of Wal-Mart, the U.S. minimum wage is "out of date with the times. We can see first-hand at Wal-Mart how many of our customers are struggling to get by. Our customers simply don't have the money to buy basic necessities between pay checks."[17] By contrast, Great Britain, whose output per capita is one-third lower than U.S. output per capita, raised its minimum wage to £5.35 in 2006, nearly twice the value of the U.S. minimum at the exchange rate of the pound for the dollar. Australia, another English-speaking country with institutions similar to those in the United States, also had a much higher minimum wage in 2006 than the United States. The fall in the real value of the minimum wage underlies the drop in real earnings for persons in the lowest 10 percent of earners in the United States, particularly low-paid women and younger workers.

Globalization in the form of increased trade with low-wage developing countries, such as China, also tends to raise inequality. Trade with a developing country increases inequality in the United States because consumers buy imports made in that low-wage country instead of more expensive products made by low-wage Americans, depressing the demand for the low-skilled American workers, and because the United States exports high-tech goods and services produced by higher-paid and more-skilled workers, raising demand for their services. Immigration also affects the supply-demand balance between high-paid and low-paid workers. The huge influx of low-skilled workers, many of whom came to the United States illegally, has increased the supply of low-skilled workers. In 1991, while the debate over the North American Free Trade Agreement (NAFTA) raged, George Borjas, Lawrence Katz, and I estimated that trade contributed perhaps 10 percent of the fall in the earnings of high school dropouts relative to better-educated workers over the previous decade and that immigration contributed 15 percent to the fall in relative earnings among dropouts.[18] We viewed those estimates as modest and were surprised when some trade economists attacked them as large. Trade theory predicts that trade creates losers as well as winners in a country, but trade specialists did not want anyone to admit that NAFTA would harm any U.S. worker for fear that the opponents of NAFTA would use this admission to rouse greater support for their cause. Continued growth of imports from low-wage countries and the continued flow of low-skill immigrants suggest that our estimates would be low for the mid-2000s.

One other market development contributed to the rise in inequality: the *deceleration* in the growth of the number of workers with bachelor's or postbaccalaureate degrees relative to the rest of the workforce. As noted, in the 1970s the rapid increase in the college-graduate workforce depressed college earnings and reduced that dimension of inequality. During the 1980s and 1990s, the college-graduate workforce continued to grow, but more slowly. De-

51

celeration of the growth of the supply meant that if demand were increasing at the same pace in the two periods, earnings inequality would increase. I attribute about 30 percent of the rise in income differences between university graduates and high school graduates to the slowdown in the growth of the college-educated workforce. But the increased income differential between university and high school graduates explains only 10 percent of the overall increase in inequality as measured by the ratio of the earnings of persons at the ninetieth percentile to those at the tenth percentile.

The observant reader will notice that these comparisons mix different measures of inequality rather than treating a single measure. This is because studies often try to link the factor to the type of inequality on which it is likely to have the greatest impact. All of the factors taken together, however, cannot explain the full rise in inequality. The reason is that most of the increase in inequality occurred within identifiable groups of workers rather than between them.

Finally, the mode of executive pay setting—management appointing boards of directors who determine executive pay in consultation with the compensation firms that management hires—contributed to the rise of inequality at the top of the earnings distribution. Ideally, boards of directors set executive pay and award stock options to give top executives incentives to make decisions that improve firm performance. But in the 1990s, many boards did not keep close account of how management reported earnings and seemed more concerned with funneling large sums to their fellow executives than with looking after shareholder interests, along lines that I examine in detail in chapter 7. In this area, U.S. exceptionalism seems to consist largely of giving top executives exceptional slack to affect their own pay.

All told, there is no single villain (if you are among the 90 percent of Americans whose real wages did not rise over the period) or hero (or if you are one of the lucky millionaires or billionaires) to explain why market wage determination produced such high levels of inequality. Several factors operated in the same direction. Some affected the relative earnings of workers by skill. Others affected the dispersion of pay within skill groups. Some reduced the pay for low-income and middle-income workers. Others increased the pay of those at the top of the distribution. That the bulk of inequality takes the form of income differences among people with the same observable characteristics makes it hard to reach a definitive economics accounting.

Inconclusive debates about the causes of the rise of inequality should not, however, deter us from looking for cures for the problem. Policies that ameliorate inequality do not have to operate on causes. If technological change is the main cause of the rise in inequality (which I doubt), that does not mean we should destroy computers. Just as we use glasses or contact lenses to cure myopia without addressing its root causes, be they genetic or environmental, we can act to reverse the massive rise in inequality without fully understanding the forces behind that rise . . . if we want to.

Should We Act to Reverse Income Inequality?

Should you care that the U.S. income distribution has gone awry?

I think you should, even if you are one of the lucky beneficiaries of rising inequality. One reason you should care is that the high level of inequality has resulted in more Americans living below the poverty line than would have been the case if the income distribution had not widened so massively. In other words, the United States, alone among the advanced countries, lost its war on poverty. In 1959 over one in five Americans lived in a family with income below the poverty line. In the 1960s, GDP per capita increased by 33 percent and, with no increase in inequality, poverty fell to 12.1 percent in 1969. Then, as inequality rose, poverty stopped falling. In the recession of the early 1980s, poverty rose to 15.2 percent—over one in six Americans had an income below the poverty line. In the recession of the early 1990s, poverty was 15.1 percent. The boom of the 1990s reduced the poverty rate to 11.3 percent in 2000, modestly lower than in 1969, but then poverty rose to 12.7 percent in 2004.[19] With GDP per capita 60 percent higher in 2005 than in 1969, the rate of poverty was higher as well! A wealthier country with more poor citizens is what rising inequality means.

But perhaps you are skeptical about the government's measures of poverty. The poverty rates I use measure absolute poverty—the proportion of people with incomes below a *fixed poverty line*. With this measure, when national income per capita rises and inequality does not increase, the proportion in poverty falls. If the income of everyone in the United States were to double, for instance, poverty would fall. By contrast, a measure of *relative poverty*—such as, say, the proportion of persons earning less than half of median earnings—would show no decline in poverty even though the poor can buy twice as much as they could before. Measures of relative poverty are in fact measures of inequality, not of living standards compared to a fixed standard.

Still, you might wonder, what does absolute poverty mean in the highest-income country in the world? The poorest Americans have electricity and stoves and refrigerators. Ninety-three percent have color televisions, 72 percent have washing machines, and 50 percent have clothes dryers. Seventy-seven percent own a car or truck. By some standards, almost no one in the United States is really poor. Only the people living in lower-income developing countries are really poor.

Granting that the poorest Americans are better off than the poorest Venezuelans or Bangladeshis or South Africans, poverty still has substantive meaning in the United States. It means first and foremost that poor persons and their families are at regular risk of losing the most basic services for modern life. In the 1990s, one-third of persons classified as poor could not pay the full amount of their gas, electric, or oil bills. One in eleven had the service turned off as a result. Sixteen percent had their telephone service disconnected because they could not pay the bill. Nearly one-quarter had no telephone at all. As for living quarters, one in four poor families could not pay the full amount of their rent or mortgage in a given year; 2 percent were evicted from their dwelling as a result. Approximately half a million poor persons are homeless—a number that has been roughly constant since the 1983 recession produced a huge spike in homelessness that shocked the country. Many poor persons live in crowded apartments with upkeep problems in dangerous neighborhoods. One-quarter of poor families report that conditions where they live are so bad that they would like to move.

Twenty percent report that they are afraid to go out in their neighborhood.[20]

Finally, at the height of the dot-com boom in 1998, some 36 million people, over one-third of them children, lived in households that the U.S. Department of Agriculture said suffered from "food insecurity"—they lacked access to food to meet basic needs just short of outright hunger. This is 10 percent of American households! Presumably these were the persons who flocked to the emergency food shelters that provided food for 25 million people that year. In addition, about 10 million persons lived in households suffering outright hunger at some point in the year—about 4 percent of the population.[21]

Thus, when you think of U.S. poverty, think of insecurity in making ends meet. Poor families spend two-thirds of their annual income on food, shelter, and utilities. In 1992–1993, this meant they could only spend about $600 on clothing, $1200 for transportation, and just over $300 for health care. Any unexpected problem—sickness, an accident, a broken appliance—becomes a financial disaster when a family is living on the margin. Insecurity and poor living conditions are associated with poor health, and indeed the poor live shorter and less healthy lives than other Americans. They are more likely to suffer from nervous breakdowns and to have heart attacks. Poor mothers are about twice as likely to have low-birthweight babies and preterm births and over 50 percent more likely to suffer infant deaths at birth. Someone in the lower part of the U.S. income distribution has five years less life expectancy than someone in the upper part of the income distribution.[22]

Finally, when you think of poverty in the United States, think of children. Poverty is more prevalent among U.S. children than among children in other advanced countries. Children in the lowest 20 percent of the U.S. income distribution are absolutely poorer than children in the lowest 20 percent of the income distribution of fifteen other advanced countries. But the flip side is that the children in the upper quintile of distribution of income are richer than children in the upper quintile in those same countries.[23]

In short, you do not have to be a lefty leftover from the student protests of the 1970s or a sociologist to see that, yes, the failure of the United States to reduce the rate of poverty with forty years of economic growth is truly a problem that the country should seek to cure.

Full Employment to the Rescue?

The 1990s boom was the ideal time for the U.S. labor market to reduce income inequality and poverty. Unemployment fell to its lowest level in years, and the proportion of adults employed was at a historic peak. The real earnings of workers increased throughout the earnings distribution and throughout the economy—in low-wage industries, such as retail trade and services, and in low-wage occupations, such as food preparers and handlers, cleaners, and laborers. Wages increased by about 10 percent among persons in the bottom 10 percent of the earnings distribution. If there was a time for the rising tide to lift the insecure rowboat of the poor and reduce poverty, this was it.[24]

Indeed, poverty did fall noticeably in the 1990s. It went down by 3.8 percentage points. But the rate of poverty of persons remained in double digits. Examining the link between economic growth and poverty in 2001, I concluded that by itself full employment and economic growth could not reduce poverty below 10 percent or so.[25] The reason is that many of the residual poor have attributes that keep them out of the job market or limit the hours they can work and their earnings. One-fifth of the poor in 1999 were disabled; 15 percent were sixty-four years of age or older; 44 percent had less than a high school education; 20 percent were taking care of elderly or disabled relatives; and so on. For persons with mental or physical disabilities, not even full employment with rising wages will bring their incomes above poverty.

My conclusion from this evidence is that the United States cannot rely exclusively on full employment to improve the living standards of the most disadvantaged and reduce poverty. It has to do something for the most disadvantaged. When I gave this message at a conference in Wisconsin in May 2000, I was sharply criticized by my discussant, a staffer for the Joint Economic Committee. My conclusion showed that I did not have faith in the power of American capitalism to resolve all economic problems without government intervention. He was right. I do not have that faith. Economics is not about faith in the unfettered market to resolve all problems. It is about learning the reality of how markets operate and what they can and cannot do.

Conclusion

As the title of this chapter states, distribution matters. At the levels of inequality found in the United States, it matters a lot. The market forces on which the United States relies extensively to determine wages produce greater and more rapidly rising inequality than in economies that rely more on institutions to determine wages. Poverty is unlikely to drop much below 10 percent even under extended full employment, which means that further reductions in poverty almost certainly will require government or private programs to help the disadvantaged outside the job market. The high level of inequality or poverty is not a clear and present danger to the country, as was racial discrimination in the 1950s and 1960s, but it is unhealthy for American ideals of political classlessness and shared citizenship. The term "two Americas"—one America in which the low-paid struggle and another America in which a small number of super-wealthy persons have huge earnings and amass giant wealth, while the middle class gets squeezed in between—was made famous by John Edwards during the 2004 presidential campaign. It is more than political rhetoric. It is reality. Distribution matters.

❧ CHAPTER 4 ❧

WHY AMERICANS WORK AND WORK

A mericans work more hours than persons in any other advanced economy. In 2005 American adults averaged 1,804
hours worked over the year compared to 1,638 hours worked by
Europeans and 1,775 hours worked by Japanese.[1]

The difference between workaholic Americans and persons in
other countries was vividly brought home to me when I helped direct a team of American and Swedish economists analyzing the
Swedish welfare state. Sweden had experienced a major economic
meltdown in 1991 and 1992 and was struggling to recover. The
team met in Chicago in the spring of 1992 to plan our joint work
over the next year. Although the Swedish economists were more in-
clined than the American economists to rely on institutions to influence outcomes (per Swedish experience), the meeting went well,
producing a general consensus about what research would be useful. To maintain the momentum I proposed that we complete first
drafts of papers over the summer and hold a workshop in Stock-
holm in September to obtain critical comments. This went down
fine with the Americans. No teaching over the summer meant lots
of time to work. An early September meeting would avoid possible
conflicts with teaching schedules.

The plan stunned the Swedes. For a few moments no one said
anything, but it was clear from the expressions on their faces that
something was amiss. Then the Swedish economist who had initiated the study stood up and explained that, unlike Americans, neither she nor any other Swede would sacrifice their five- to six-week
summer vacations to work on the papers. Some had vacation houses

in the archipelago, where they went with their families. Some had planned tourist excursions to exciting places. The Swedish economists would do their work in the fall after the summer holidays, and we would hold the workshop in December. That is what we did.

Why do Americans follow a different drummer when it comes to work than the Europeans or the Japanese? Is the U.S. culture so different from that of other countries that we prefer work to leisure? Do we take less pleasure from spending time with our families or from recreational activities than they do? Have we created an unhealthy work-family balance?

This chapter argues that America's workaholic behavior comes from the incentive generated by high inequality. High inequality is both a carrot and a stick for work. The carrot is that Americans who work hard have a better chance of being promoted, moving up in the wide distribution of earnings, and experiencing substantial earnings increases. The stick is that Americans who lose their jobs suffer greatly because the United States has a minimal safety net for the unemployed. The potential both for gain and for loss is much lower for Europeans. European earnings distributions are compressed, so that Europeans who work hard and rise in their country's earnings distribution make only modest income gains. And those who lose their jobs are protected by a generous welfare state.

In addition, the wide U.S. earnings distribution creates huge incentives for workers to choose higher-paid occupations, such as investment banking, over occupations that pay less because much of their output consists of social externalities, such as science or math; to move across country in pursuit of better jobs; to change jobs frequently; and to quit their job when they have problems at their workplace. In the United States more than in other countries, work is paramount in how people live, and that creates problems of work and family life balance.

Workaholics Run Wild

Americans are world leaders in time worked among countries with high levels of income. Peasants and workers in many impoverished countries work more hours than Americans because they could not survive otherwise. In China, migrants from rural areas to the big cities work every possible hour to make money to send back to their families. Many immigrants to the United States and other countries work long hours to establish themselves in a new environment. Among OECD countries, workers in Korea—which has not yet fully adopted the five-day workweek and where many workers are self-employed—work 32 percent more hours than Americans.[2] But Korea has barely half of U.S. GDP per capita. The American exception is working so many hours despite a high level of GDP per capita.

About half of the difference in hours worked in the United States compared to other advanced countries is due to differences in the length of vacations—two weeks in the United States compared to four to six weeks in other advanced countries. The federal government does not legislate minimum vacations for workers, as do the governments of most other countries. Unions bargain over vacations and other worker issues for just 8 percent of private-sector workers. As a result, competitive market forces determine the vacation time of most workers. But the gap between the United States and other countries in vacation time lies not simply in the length of the vacations of most workers. Even when Americans have vacation days, many do not take their full vacation time. One study found that in 1992 the average American employee took twelve out of fourteen days of vacation time. The more job insecurity the respondent reported, the fewer days of vacation that person took.[3]

Americans also work more hours per day than persons in other countries and take less time off for sickness, maternity, and other personal issues. U.S. legislation has established the normal workday as eight hours and imposes a time-and-a-half charge on employers for hours worked beyond that. This is one of the rare cases where U.S. rules are more restrictive than European rules. Many European countries allow workers to put in more hours with no extra charge by letting them substitute extra hours one day for fewer hours another day. In any case, overtime rates average around 20 percent above normal rates. But even with high overtime rates, most U.S. firms prefer to work existing staff longer hours than to hire new staff. The reason is that firms incur large health insurance costs when they bring on new permanent employees. In the European Union, the state provides health insurance through taxation so that health insurance does not influence firms in deciding whether to extend the hours of existing staff or to hire new staff.

The advent of the computer and the Internet has further increased the amount of time Americans work. In 2004 the 10.2 million workers who reported that they did unpaid work at home in addition to paid work at their workplace averaged 6.8 hours of additional work—essentially an extra day for which they were not reimbursed beyond their normal pay.[4] With email and the digitalization of white-collar work, it is easy to do some tasks at home after hours. The incentive for putting in the extra time is that by completing or improving projects, you increase your chances of being promoted or keeping your job if the firm has to lay off workers.

The time spent at work by American women is a major part of American workaholism. American women are more likely to be fully employed than women in most other advanced countries. This is true even when they have small children. As pointed out in chapter 2, American women accomplish this by buying the market equivalent of household goods and services to make up for their reduced time producing traditional household goods. Because they spend less time doing housework, taking care of children, and helping elderly or sick relatives, they work more over the year—and experience more stress in trying to balance family considerations and their work lives.

Volunteering

With all the time they spend working for pay and the incentive to put in extra hours on the job, whether at the office or at home, you might think that Americans would have little time or energy for volunteer work. But Americans lead the world in volunteer work activities as well. Between 10 and 15 percent of Americans volunteer in a given week, during which time they work about seven hours—or nearly another day of work. Another 15 percent report having volunteered at some time over the year. I estimate that volunteer time adds 3 to 4 percent to the total time worked in the United States. Given the modest volunteering rates in other countries, treating volunteer time as work increases the difference between U.S. and foreign time worked by 2 to 3 percent.[5]

From the perspective of the opportunity cost of time, volunteers should be low-skilled or unemployed persons, whose time is less valuable than that of high-skilled employed persons. The facts show the opposite. Volunteer workers are usually full-time employees with high wages. The typical volunteer has two years of education beyond high school, and 40 percent of volunteers are managers or professionals—nearly double the managerial and professional share of the workforce. Many use their work skills at their volunteer activity. The CEO volunteer raises funds from the wealthy, the computer expert volunteer runs the IT system of the homeless shelter, and so on.[6] Without volunteering, the United States would need a larger public sector and taxes or suffer considerable loss of charitable, cultural, and educational activities.

Again, from the perspective of the opportunity cost of time, we might expect that volunteers would be persons without children, whose upbringing takes considerable time and energy. The facts show the opposite. Volunteers have larger family sizes than nonvolunteers. Adults with children volunteer more than others, giving time to activities—parent-teacher association meetings, scouting, coaching teams, and the like—that benefit their children as well as their neighbors. Reciprocal altruism—people helping others with the expectation that the others will help them in turn—may underlie this behavior. Johnny's mom volunteers to coach the soccer team on the understanding that Mary's dad will pick up the kids after school and bring them to the field or assist in some other activity. Surprisingly, persons who work long hours tend to volunteer *more* than others. This is particularly true among men. But it is flexible work schedules that are most highly linked to volunteering: workers who can rearrange their work hours, within some bounds, are far more likely to volunteer than workers with less control over their work schedules.[7]

Culture and Attitudes

If Americans were workaholics for reasons lying deep in the American culture and psyche, the United States should have generated greater work time than other countries for much of the twentieth century. But in the 1960s and 1970s, Americans worked modestly fewer hours than persons in many European countries and many fewer hours than the Japanese. Labor participation rates in the United States in 1970 were about average for an advanced country. The United States introduced the forty-hour workweek earlier than other countries and made vacation time a normal part of compensation in collective bargaining right after the end of World War II. But as real wages increased in other countries while they stagnated or fell in the United States, and as inequality here increased, the country moved to the head of the pack in hours worked. When the United States surpassed Japan in hours worked in the 1990s, it made newspaper headlines.[8] The change in the United States from working a bit less than other countries to becoming the workaholic of advanced economies argues against any cultural interpretation of U.S. working time behavior.

Americans do have different attitudes about work than persons in other countries in some respects. Americans are more likely than Europeans to say that people are rewarded for their effort and less likely to say that inequality benefits the rich.[9] They are also more likely than Europeans to say that they work "as best I can even if it interferes with the rest of my life" rather than that they work hard, "but not if it interferes with life or only as hard as I have to."[10] In a 2006 survey that asked respondents to rate themselves between 1 and 5 where 1 meant they worked "not very hard" and 5 meant they worked "very hard," one-half of Americans gave themselves a 5, and 31 percent gave themselves a 4.[11] Asked if they wanted to work more hours, fewer hours, or the same hours at their current rate of pay, Americans were more likely than Europeans to say they wanted to work more.[12]

Indeed, a majority of Americans who work fifty to fifty-five hours a week report that they want to work more hours as opposed to working fewer hours. Not until Americans work over sixty

63

hours does the proportion who want to work fewer hours exceed the proportion who want to work more hours.[13]

Because the experiences of individuals at work influence their attitudes toward work time just as their attitudes affect their experiences, I do not look favorably at efforts to use observed differences in attitudes to explain differences in work time. But if I were less queasy about treating attitudes as an independent factor and tried to explain the hours-worked difference between Americans and Europeans in terms of differences in attitudes, I would still be unable to explain most of the U.S.-EU difference in hours worked.

If culture and attitudes do not explain why Americans work, work, work, what does?

It's the Incentives, St——

The most plausible explanation is that U.S. behavior reflects the incentives that the labor market gives persons to work. Historically, low-paid workers have worked longer hours than high-paid workers because long hours were necessary to make ends meet. The phrase "idle rich" reflects social reality half a century or more ago. In 1950 Americans in the top decile of the wage distribution worked fewer hours than those in the lower parts of the wage distribution. As wages increased more rapidly for workers at the top of the distribution relative to those at the bottom of the distribution, this pattern changed. Groups with sizable increases in wages increased their work time, while those whose wages stagnated worked less. By 2005, Americans in the top decile of the wage distribution worked more hours than those in the bottom decile.[14] This reversal in the relation between time worked and pay implies that the incentive to work extra hours due to higher earnings per hour (the substitution effect) overwhelmed the tendency to spend higher income on leisure (the income effect).

Consistent with this interpretation, hours worked are greater in occupations with high inequality of pay, where there is a greater payoff to moving up in the earnings distribution (by working more hours or harder) than in occupations with low inequality of pay.[15] Similarly, looking across countries, those with greater inequality of pay have higher hours worked than those with lower inequality of pay. The United States is in the top spot in both inequality and hours. In addition, workers in countries with greater inequality are more likely to prefer an increase in their time worked and the accompanying higher earnings than workers in countries with lower inequality, who prefer lower work time and earnings and the greater leisure that brings.[16]

Does the positive association between inequality and hours worked mean that inequality always increases effort and output?

When I first wondered about this, I thought the answer was "yes": more inequality leads to more work. But then I thought about how inequality in grading students would affect the amount of time students spend studying. If I announced that regardless of their performance on exams or assignments everyone in the class would receive a gentleman's B (a grade-inflated gentleman's C), what kind of effort might I expect from the class? Introspection and discussions with students made clear that the answer would be "not much." Students would allocate time to classes where effort could improve their grade and away from classes where grades were given independent of effort.

Alternatively, what would happen if I announced that I would give an A to the top-scoring student and fail everyone else? This would be the maximum possible inequality in grades. Since most students would lack the skills to compete for the top grade, they would probably give up and do no work for the class. Again, they would deem it better to study for courses in which they had a chance of succeeding than for a course in which, no matter what they did, they probably would fail. On the other hand, the top two to three students in the class might work exceptionally hard. For this reason, the high-inequality grading system should lead to greater output than giving a B grade to everyone regardless of performance score.

Finally, what would happen if I used a normal grade curve—say, one-quarter A grades, one-half B grades of some form, and one-quarter C grades or less? Because the normal grade curve gives incentives to persons at all points of the ability distribution to do better, it should lead to the greatest effort by students and the greatest

65

number of correct answers on a final examination. Following this line of thinking, I concluded that inequality should affect output with an inverse-U pattern and that medium inequality would produce the greatest effort. Economic theorists have come to a similar conclusion in analyzing how rational people should behave when they compete in a tournament for prizes.[17] It is better when those running the tournament give several prizes of varying value rather than one big prize.

But introspection and theory can do no more than provide clues to economic behavior. Only observations of behavior can tell fact from fancy. Since Harvard would not allow me to experiment with different grade schemes in a real class setting (the extreme inequality grading scheme risked student protests, and the gentleman's B would no doubt have emptied the class), I decided to use a laboratory experiment to test the idea that, up to a point, inequality generates effort—and by proxy, hours worked—and then after that point it reduces effort. Not so long ago, psychologists did most of the laboratory experiments in the social sciences while economists preferred to examine behavior in the field or sit in their offices and theorize. But today economists have learned the value of testing ideas about behavior under laboratory conditions as well.

The Inequality/Incentive Maze Experiment

In the inequality/incentive experiment, participants were asked to solve mazes in a two-round process.[18] The maze was a good design to examine the effects of varying levels of inequality and incentives because the ability to solve mazes differs considerably among people. In the first round, everyone was given a modest piece rate for each maze they solved; this round revealed who was good or bad at the maze-solving task. In the second round, subjects were asked to solve mazes in a tournament in which six participants competed for prizes. There were three prize schedules. In the high-inequality schedule, $30 was given to the person who scored the most and $0 to everyone else. This was the equivalent of giving an A to the best student and an F to everyone else. In the no-inequality schedule, $5 was given to each of the six participants regardless of the number of mazes they solved. This was equivalent to the gentleman's B solution. In the medium-inequality schedule, $15 was given to the subject who solved the highest number of mazes, $8 to the subject solving the next highest number, $4 to the next, $2 to the next, and $1 to the person who scored next to last. This was the equivalent of the normal grading curve.

In the key experiment, we posted the number of mazes solved in the first round of the experiment so that everyone knew their rank relative to others in their group. Thus, the lower scorers in the first round would know that they had little chance to win the top prize in the high-inequality experiment but might earn a few dollars extra by improving their position in the medium-inequality experiment. By contrast, the highest scorers in round 1 would know that in the high-inequality treatment they had a reasonable chance to win $30, and that would give them an incentive of $30 to put out full effort. In the medium-inequality experiment, the incentive for scoring first rather than second was less ($15, $8, or $7), but still substantial. Everyone knew they would get nothing more by solving more mazes in the no-inequality treatment, so their effort there would depend solely on intrinsic motivation.

Figure 4.1 shows the results of this experiment in terms of the change in output for groups of six participants between the first round, when everyone had the same piece-rate incentive, and the second round, when we gave different groups one of the three incentive treatments. The figure displays an inverse U. Output is lowest in the no-incentive case, rises to a maximum in the medium-inequality case, and then falls in the maximum-inequality case. The implication is that an economy gains more output when it gives incentives to people throughout the distribution of ability than when the bulk of the rewards go to the person at the top.

Unexpectedly, another form of economic behavior manifested itself in our experiment. The incentives to solve mazes induced subjects to cheat (shades of the Enron scandal and other business and financial behavior scandals that made headlines in the early 2000s). We told subjects to finish every maze before going on to solve the next maze. But when they could earn more by breaking our rule, some did that. They skipped a maze and proceeded to report all of

Figure 4.1   Number of Mazes Solved Increased Most with
Medium Inequality of Rewards in Laboratory
Experiment

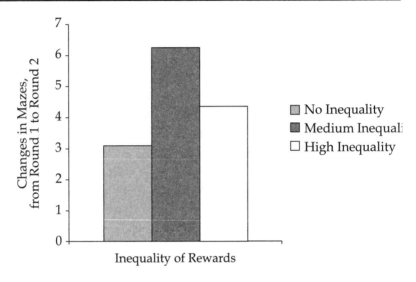

Inequality of Rewards

Source: Richard Freeman and Alex Gelber, "Optimal Inequality/Incentives: A Laboratory Experiment," working paper 12588 (Cambridge, Mass.: National Bureau of Economic Research, October 2006).

the mazes as solved, including those after the skipped maze. Some jumped their pencil over a line and claimed to have solved that maze. The behavior of the subjects who cheated provided a serendipitous test of responsiveness to incentives: lo and behold, the pattern of cheating also followed an inverse U. In the high-inequality experiment, people with high first-round scores and a chance of winning the top prize tended to cheat, but in the medium-inequality treatment people throughout the distribution cheated. Financial incentives motivate dishonest effort as well as honest effort. Boards of directors and compensation experts who give huge incentives to executives, take notice.

Dishonesty aside, the big rewards the United States offers to high flyers and the low safety net it holds out to those who do badly in the labor market create larger incentives for work throughout the earnings distribution than in other advanced countries. This does not mean that the United States has found the optimum inequality for inducing effort. Some of the huge inequality in the United States is due to luck or to the position of one's family and could be eliminated without affecting effort. And as the maze experiment showed, high inequality can discourage effort among those with little chance of gaining high earnings. Americans worked as long and hard at the lower Ronald Reagan level of inequality as they do at the higher level of the mid-2000s, and they worked hardest during World War II when inequality was even lower. I would bet that the country could generate as much or even more effort and output if it increased income and incentives in lower parts of the distribution and lowered income and incentives at the top, but perhaps I have an exalted view of the work ethic of those at the top.

Investing in Education and Careers

There is another way in which inequality affects labor market behavior. The income differences between more-educated and more-skilled workers and less-educated and less-skilled workers give people an incentive to invest in education and training.

The U.S. higher education system operates according to market principles. Hundreds of universities and over two thousand colleges compete for students, for funding, and for faculty and other resources. They offer courses and curricula that respond to what students want, and what students want in turn reflects the skills that they believe will get them good jobs in the labor market.[19] As a result, enrollments in the United States vary among fields in response to labor market incentives. In some fields, enrollments oscillate between large numbers of students, which increase the supply of graduates and depress earnings several years later, and smaller numbers, which decrease supply and increase earnings three to four years later. This "cobweb pattern" is most pronounced in engineering and other fields where the link between field and occupation is strongest. In other fields, enrollments rise or fall over long periods, with trend changes in the pay and employment opportunities for graduates in those areas. From the 1970s through the 2000s, the biggest trend in enrollments was toward master's degrees in business administration, reflecting the great demand for MBAs in the business world.

The high responsiveness of Americans to income incentives and the large income difference between college graduates and less-educated workers suggests that the United States should be the world leader in the proportion of young persons in college. For many years this was the case, but in the 1990s several EU countries, Japan, and Korea surpassed the United States in college-going. In 2002 the United States ranked ninth among advanced countries in the proportion of young people going to university. The reason is that the incentive to invest in higher education depends on tuition and fees as well as on the earnings advantage of going to college. Tuition and fees are higher in the United States than in the rest of the world; in other advanced countries, governments often make university training free for anyone who qualifies. The huge income inequality in the United States makes it difficult for many low-income students to finance a four-year college degree.

In the 2000s, leaders of high-tech firms, including Microsoft's Bill Gates and top persons in the nation's scientific and educational establishment, raised concerns that too few U.S. students were choosing science and engineering for the economic health of the country. Some believed that the country had to revamp its entire school system to increase the supply of talent in science and engineering. In a society where educational decisions are made by the state, this might be the appropriate strategy. But the responsiveness of Americans to market incentives suggests that the shortfall of students entering these fields largely reflects weak labor market incentives to choose science and engineering careers. Consider, for example, the incentive to earn a PhD in biology versus earning an MBA or MD. In 2005 students considering a PhD in biology could expect to study for six or more years to earn their degree and then spend three or more years working a postdoc before entering a shaky job market. By contrast, their classmate who got an MBA could earn much more after just two additional years of schooling. MDs could expect to earn $1 million more over their lifetime than PhDs in biology. In the 1990s through 2005, earnings in science and engineering occupations increased less rapidly than in many other high-level occupations. If the United States truly wants to attract more young Americans into science and engineering, moral suasion will not do the trick. It is necessary to increase the economic incentives to study in these areas.

There are many studies of how student career choices respond to economic incentives.[20] One of the most striking examples is the response of science and engineering students to the decision by the National Science Foundation (NSF) to double the value of its fellowships to graduate students from $15,000 in 1999 to $30,000 in 2005. I have heard two stories about why NSF increased the amounts. According to one, the increase resulted from a report by an oversight committee that said NSF fellowships were too low and in danger of losing their prestige as the premier graduate fellowship. The other story was that a congressman told the head of the agency that his son/daughter could not make ends meet on an NSF graduate research fellowship and that NSF had better raise the amounts if it wanted his support for a higher NSF budget. Whatever the cause, the supply response to the doubling of the value of the awards was huge. The number of students applying for the stipend increased from 4,799 in 1999 to 8,939 in 2004.[21] Many of the additional applicants had superb qualifications, which allowed NSF to give awards to persons with stronger observable qualifications, in the form of higher GRE scores, better letters of recommendation, and so on, than in the past. As another indicator of supply responsiveness, in 2006 a survey at Harvard asked students who were not majoring in science and engineering how they would respond if science and engineering majors obtained $20,000 scholarships. Fourteen percent reported that they would switch into that area. Since approximately 18 percent of Harvard students were majoring in science and engineering, this response would have increased the number of graduates with science and engineering degrees by nearly 80 percent! Nearly 40 percent of students said they would pursue graduate studies if they won a national fellowship for $40,000 per year.[22] My response to complaints about Americans not being good enough or interested enough to go into science and engineering is to say: pay more first and then see what happens.

Work and Family-Life Balance

Working long hours creates potential conflicts in families with children, particularly when both spouses work. In past decades, female labor force participation dipped in the child-rearing years as women shifted from working in the market to taking care of children in the home. Leaving the workforce for a number of years invariably produced lower future earnings and less career success. In the 1990s and 2000s, however, most U.S. women who bore children remained in the workforce and struggled to balance family life and work in a labor market in which career structures and workaholic incentives had been developed for a workforce of prime (male) breadwinners who could work endlessly while relying on a (female) partner to keep the family hearth going. These structures and incentives do not fit in the new world of dual family earners.

The problems faced by women in academic careers highlight the difficulty of combining career and family in such a world. In academia, employers make tenure decisions when faculty are in their late thirties or early forties on the basis of publications and output. When female academics have a child, they typically reduce their hours at work and thus obtain fewer research findings and write fewer papers; as a result, their chances for gaining tenure are also reduced. By contrast, male faculty often increase their hours of work when their wife has a child, which has the opposite effect on their chances of tenure. Many women feel pressured to choose between family and work. In the science and engineering occupations that I have studied, there is an outflow of highly capable women into less time-demanding and less stressful occupations, which potentially reduces the quality of faculty in these fields.[23] With more women than men graduating from colleges, and with women making up large proportions of master's graduates, doctorate graduates, and professional degree recipients in law, medicine, and business, the sluggish career progression of a large proportion of the best-educated American workers creates a societal problem.

In response to the new working situation, some firms have developed family-friendly work policies (flextime, provision of day care facilities at workplaces, and so on). They adopt these policies not out of the goodness of their hearts but because they can make more money if they attract and retain female talent. Some firms have embraced tele-working, which allows employees to work at home at least part of the time; this arrangement saves on office space as well. But other firms have done little in this area. I expect that the U.S. labor market will experiment with alternative ways to keep American women (and men) working and working and working for some time to come.

Conclusion: Rat Race or Virtuous Labor?

Should we lament American workaholism as excessive time worked due to an economic rat race or applaud it as the bedrock for American economic opportunity and success?

The answer lies in part in the inequality and incentives that motivate persons to work long hours and to choose their careers and lifestyles. If, as in the 1980s through the mid-2000s, Americans work hard and can barely keep their economic heads above water while the super-rich obtain the bulk of the rewards from economic growth, I would view workaholic behavior as a prisoner's dilemma problem due to the failure of workers to coordinate their work times: every individual gains by working long hours, but all workers lose by the collective pattern of long hours of work. The analogy is with people standing on their tiptoes at a parade. If you are the only person on your toes, you get a better view. But if everyone stands up on their toes, no one gets a better view. The responsiveness of career and educational choices to economic incentives underlies some of the dynamism of the U.S. labor market and economy, though it too can be excessive.

If the responsiveness of U.S. employees to inequalities in pay within and across occupations produces greater growth, which

73

raises their income in the future, then U.S. workaholic behavior and economic responsiveness would look more like the bedrock of economic opportunity. A change in government tax or spending policy that reduced inequality (for instance, a greater Earned Income Tax Credit [EITC] and higher taxes on the super-wealthy) or a spurt in unionism that shifted pay from executives to employees could test the two interpretations and illuminate the link between inequality, incentives, and time worked better than our lab experiment. If increased scholarships and fellowship support induced more students to enter science and engineering fields—or, more broadly, to attend college—and this produced a burst of innovation and growth, then high responsiveness to incentives would be virtuous. If instead this flooded the job market and drove down earnings and opportunities so that many left their areas of expertise, the labor market would benefit from less responsiveness. In any case, the message of this chapter is that the high inequality in earnings in the United States and the high work effort by Americans are interrelated phenomena: we cannot change one without changing the other.

✃ CHAPTER 5 ✃

WHERE HAVE ALL THE UNIONS GONE . . . LONG TIME PASSING?

Trade unions are the primary worker institution in capitalist economies. They replace market wage setting with collective bargaining and management control over workplaces with "industrial jurisprudence"—rules and negotiated procedures to deal with workplace problems. They guarantee workers a voice at the workplace and make sure that management hears workers' views on issues.

For the past half-century, unions have been dying in the United States. Year after year, the proportion of wage and salary workers in unions has fallen. In 2005 union density in the private sector was 7.9 percent of employed wage and salary workers—comparable to the level in the 1880s. Density in the public sector was 36.4 percent; this is over four times the private-sector level, but the public sector accounts for just 15 percent of the U.S. workforce.[1] As a result, economywide density was 12.5 percent. But it could go lower. In the state with the lowest rate of unionization, North Carolina, density fell from 5.3 percent in 1990 to 2.7 percent in 2005.[2] Because the United States does not extend collective bargaining contracts beyond the signatories, the low level of membership translates into the smallest proportion of workers covered by collective bargaining among advanced countries. In response to the failure of the AFL-CIO to find a way to reverse the decline in membership, some large trade unions left the federation in 2005 to form Change to Win, a trade union coalition dedicated to organizing new workers.

Why have unions lost representation in the private sector? What are the consequences for workers and the economy? Can unions rise like the phoenix from the ashes, or is the United States on the verge of reaching the union-free environment that anti-union zealots have long hoped for?

This chapter tells the story of the decline of unionism in the United States and offers radical suggestions on how to give workers collective voice to represent their interests despite this decline. I began researching unionism in the 1980s and have done more work on unions than on any other topic. My 1984 book *What Do Unions Do?* (with James Medoff) has been the center of union research since its publication. In 2004–2005 the *Journal of Labor Research* held a twentieth-anniversary review in which two dozen or so researchers assessed the book's findings and arguments in light of ensuing analysis and events. The symposium led to *What Do Unions Do? A Twenty-Year Perspective*, which is much larger than the original.[3] To my relief, the review concluded that the work had stood the test of time, which is more than can be said for the union movement. In 2007 Beijing University Press will publish a Chinese edition as one of the modern classics in economics. But is *What Do Unions Do?* about a live institution, or is it paleontology about a dinosaur that has failed the market test in the United States?

The Falling House of Labor

The United States has a checkered record with unions. Employers have violently opposed worker efforts to unionize in the past. Courts have challenged the right of workers to unionize even after Congress enacted legislation meant to legitimize unions. On the union side, the United States is the only advanced country where the mob has run major unions, ripping off workers and firms, as the movie *On the Waterfront* highlighted in 1954. During the Depression, Congress enacted the National Labor Relations Act to move the struggle to unionize from the streets and factories to the ballot box. If a majority of workers voted for a union to represent them, firms had to recognize and bargain with that union. Many workers voted for unions in government-sponsored elections during the Depression and World War II and the Korean War, and many joined unions without going through the process. In 1955, when the AFL and CIO merged into a single federation, 37 percent of private-sector workers were unionized, and many non-union firms mimicked union agreements to keep their workers from joining unions. It was the era of Big Labor.

Whether union representation of the workforce increases or decreases over time is determined by the number of new workers organized by unions minus the number they lose owing to the closure or shrinkage of unionized workplaces and the growth of the workforce. When the workforce grows, unions must organize more workers to maintain their share of employment even if no members leave. Assuming roughly constant attrition of membership and growth of the workforce, the key factor in how union density changes is the number of workers organized by unions relative to the workforce. From the mid-1950s through the mid-1960s, unions organized from 0.5 percent to 0.7 percent of the private-sector workforce through National Labor Relations Board elections. This fell short of the rate of organizing needed to maintain union density, but that did not trouble union leaders, since unions were expanding greatly into the public sector. In 1972 AFL-CIO head George Meany dismissed concerns about organizing new workers: "I don't know, I don't care. . . . Why should we worry about organizing groups of people who do not appear to want to be organized? . . . I used to worry about . . . the size of the membership. . . . I stopped worrying because to me it doesn't make any difference. . . . The organized fellow is the fellow that counts."[4] Foresight was not one of Meany's virtues.

In the 1970s and 1980s, the proportion of the workforce in union electoral victories fell to less than 0.2 percent.[5] These statistics imply a massive drop in union density over time. Why was the rate of organization falling? Could anything be done to make it easier for workers to be organized? I went to Lane Kirkland, Meany's successor as head of the AFL-CIO, and offered to bring together diverse researchers, some friendly and some unfriendly to unions, for an academic conference on these questions. Kirkland shook his head and told me that the AFL-CIO would not cooperate with such a meeting.

He did not want to include researchers unfriendly to unionism. And academic studies were not important in any case. He was going to use the union's political clout to get Congress to enact labor law reform that would make it easier to organize workers.

In the 1990s and early 2000s, the proportion of the workforce organized through elections fell below 0.1 percent, or barely 100,000 workers unionized per year; in an economy with some 145 million workers, that is effectively no one. Unions gained more members outside the electoral process, but still not enough to staunch the fall in density. At last, union leaders recognized that the decline was spelling the death of unionism in the United States. In 1995 national union leaders forced Kirkland to resign and elected John Sweeney to invigorate organizing efforts.[6] Sweeney's "New Voice" team called for unions to spend larger shares of their revenues on organizing. Some unions did. Some unions elected organizing directors as union presidents. But many internationals and locals did not increase their organizing budgets, while others could not find fruitful campaigns on which to spend the money they had. Union density continued to fall. In 2005 several major unions, led by the Service Employees International Union (SEIU) and the Teamsters, withdrew from the AFL-CIO because they felt the federation was incapable of reversing the decline in density. These unions set up the Change to Win coalition to increase union resources for organizing and jump-start a turnaround in union density. Perhaps competition among unions would spur more successful organizing than the unified house of labor.

Why Has Unionism Declined?

The decline of private-sector unionism is not a mechanical story of employment shifting from blue-collar mining and manufacturing, where unions had great strength, to white-collar service sectors, where unions were weaker. The fall in union density has been ubiquitous across occupations and industries in the private sector. From 1983 to 2005, density fell in durable manufacturing, in transportation, in mining, in utilities, in nondurable manufacturing, and in construction. Less than 20 percent of the decline was associated with a change in the composition of jobs.[7]

The decline in unionism is also not a mechanical story of labor supply shifting from men who join unions to women who do not, or from high school graduates who unionize to college graduates who do not.[8] In 2005 women were as likely to be union members as men, and college graduates are more likely than high school graduates or dropouts to be union members. Persons with postcollege education have over two and a half times the union density of persons with less than a high school education. Unionized workers in the United States are disproportionately teachers, nurses, airline pilots, entertainers and athletes, machinists, police, firefighters, craft workers, and other highly skilled workers. The less skilled cannot gain union representation even when they want it.

The story of the decline of unionism is an economic story about the incentives and behavior of firms, unions, and workers interacting in the framework set by U.S. labor law of the Depression era. This framework gives workers and firms a stark choice for representation: a collective bargaining union or nothing. This contrasts with the wider selection of forms of representation available in virtually all other advanced countries, including Canada. Counter to the original purpose of the National Labor Relations Act, the legal framework, as interpreted by the courts, forces the unionization issue into a conflict situation that pits unions and workers who seek unions against management.

There are three suspects for doing in the unions: management, the unions themselves, and workers. If we look for motivation, as economists generally do, the most likely suspect is management. Unions raise wages and benefits for workers in organized workplaces, and these increases lower profits. If we look for institutional competence, as organizational sociologists do, the likely suspects are the unions themselves. Union leaders failed to address declining density until it reached crisis proportions. If we look at who votes on union representation, the likely suspects are workers. Perhaps workers decided that unions did not serve their interests in the modern information economy.

It's Management

Managers in the United States fight hard against unions that seek to organize their workforces. Management campaign tactics include: making captive-audience speeches in which management orders all employees to listen to anti-union messages while forbidding union supporters to make their case; making "forecasts" (threats are illegal) that unionization will lead to closure and job loss; bombarding workers with company campaign material; denying unions access to workers on company property; and ordering supervisors to hold one-on-one anti-union meetings with workers. All of these actions are legally permissible under the National Labor Relations Act. If management is uncertain about how to fight unions, it can hire consultants simply by Googling "union prevention" or "labor-management consultants" or "union busters." Going beyond legally permissible tactics, some managers fire or illegally discipline union activists in NLRB elections. One study estimates almost one-in-five union organizers or activists can expect to be fired as a result of their activities in a union election campaign.[9]

Particular tactics aside, it is the confrontational tone that management adopts when workers seek to unionize that most strongly influences the election process. Three-quarters of workers believe that an employee organization can be effective *only if* management cooperates with it. Nearly two-thirds of workers say that they prefer an organization that has little nominal power but does have management cooperation over an organization that has "more power, but [that] management oppose[s]."[10] By letting workers know that management opposes unions and will not cooperate with any union, management can discourage worker efforts to organize.

Indicative of the effort that management puts into defeating unions, my employer, Harvard University, battled for over a decade to keep workers from unionizing. Harvard got the NRLB to change the election district for voting from the medical school, where the technicians who started the union drive worked, to the entire university workforce, which included worksites as far away as Maine. Although the president of the university, Derek Bok, was a leading labor law scholar whose writings favored collective bargaining, Harvard did everything possible to convince employees that a union would be bad for them. If nonprofit Harvard under a pro-union president battled so hard to keep unions out, imagine what profit-seeking businesses do.

Managements in other countries do not fight unions with anything like the resources and zeal of American managers, if they fight them at all. In Britain most managers are neutral when workers seek to organize.[11] If workers want to be represented by a union, it is their choice. Throughout Europe management deals with unions and accepts union efforts to sign up workers. The divergent attitude of American and European management toward unions was driven home to me in 1988, when I visited Danish union and business leaders courtesy of the labor attaché at the U.S. embassy. Because I was interested in management opposition to unions, I asked the attaché to arrange for meetings with companies opposed to unions. She said she could not do that because there were no anti-union firms. No anti-union employers? Impossible! Then take me to the small employers' association, I said, certain that small Danish firms, like their U.S. counterparts, would be in the forefront of opposition to unions. I was stunned when the Danish small business association said that they preferred to operate with collective bargaining. By negotiating wages and conditions throughout the economy, unions reduced the need for small firms to worry about those issues. Collective bargaining leveled the playing field for firms to compete on nonwage dimensions, where small employers could excel.

American and European businesses differ in their attitude toward unions not because American managers are reactionaries who reject the right of workers to form unions while Europeans are social democrats who view unions as the best thing since sliced bread. It is the economics of their situations that creates the difference in attitudes. In the United States, where unions cover only a small proportion of the workforce and bargain for higher wages, pensions, and health insurance, the unionized firm has higher costs. Management does what it can to improve productivity, but it generally cannot find ways to improve the operation of the firm enough to cover the higher costs of labor and thus ends up with lower profits. In Europe, where almost all firms pay the collectively bargained rate and health care is provided nationally, unions do not create a competitive disadvantage for an organized employer. Since unions do not affect the bottom line, why worry if workers choose to unionize?

It's the Unions

Unions are the second set of suspects for causing the decline of unionization. The unions that left the AFL-CIO in the summer of 2005 complained that the federation had done too little to galvanize organizing efforts and spent too much dues money on Washington political activity. They advocated a huge increase in organizing budgets. Such an increase is necessary for unions to have a chance of unionizing large numbers of workers. But even with additional resources, unions have to find more creative ways to gain members than battling employers at the workplace. Management opposition has raised the cost of union organizing to such an extent that unions would have to devote the bulk of their budgets to organizing to win enough workers to maintain their 2005 density, much less to increase density.[12] And as density falls, it becomes more costly for members to fund organizing campaigns big enough to raise density. The reason is arithmetic: at low levels of density, there are relatively few members to pay for the campaign and many nonmembers to organize. What the unions need is some great organizing innovation and triumph—such as convincing Wal-Mart to welcome unions—that sparks a wave of low-cost organizing success. Slogging it out with firms that have deeper pockets is unlikely to get unions much.

What Workers Want

The purpose of unions or any other workplace organization is to meet the needs of employees. It is what workers want, not what union functionaries want or what management wants, that should determine whether workers have a union or some other organization or no organization representing them at their workplace. If workers are happy with management human resource policies, legislated protections, and the option to quit a bad workplace and get a new job, there is no place for unions.[13] If workers seek some form of collective representation in dealing with workplace problems, there is a place for unions or some other worker organization in the labor market. So the key question that has motivated much research is whether or not workers want some institutional protection or collective voice at their workplace.

To answer this question, Joel Rogers and I, in what we boldly described as the "mother of all workplace surveys," asked workers in the mid-1990s about their workplace experiences and desires for union or non-union representation and participation.[14] In our Workplace Representation and Participation Survey (WRPS), we found that 32 percent of *non-union* private-sector workers wanted a trade union at their workplace and that 90 percent of union workers wanted to maintain their union. If workers had their way, private-sector union density would be on the order of 40 percent—three to four times the rate in the sample in our study. Similar surveys conducted after our study came up with higher estimates of the proportion of non-union workers who wanted unions. Figure 5.1 shows that the proportion of non-union workers who said they would vote union exceeded 50 percent in 2003 and 2005.

Our survey also asked workers about worker organizations beyond unions. More workers said that they wanted a non-union organization at their workplace to discuss issues with management than said they wanted unions. (The unions did not like this survey result.) In fact, most workers wanted an organization to be "run jointly by employees and management." Again, surveys that followed ours confirmed these findings. Hart Research Associates asked workers in 1997, 1999, and 2001: "Suppose there was a proposal to form an employees' organization that was not a union in your workplace but that would represent the interests of employees and meet regularly with management to discuss important workplace issues." Seventy-eight percent of workers said that they would definitely or probably vote for such an organization.[15] In short, not only is there unfilled demand for unions, but there is even greater unfilled demand for worker organizations to discuss issues with management outside of collective bargaining.

Figure 5.1   Likelihood of Non-union Workers Voting in Union
               Representation Election, Peter Hart Surveys,
               1984 to 2005

If an election were held tomorrow to decide whether your workplace
would have a union or not, do you think you would definitely vote for
forming a union, probably vote for forming a union, probably vote
against forming a union, or definitely vote against forming a union?

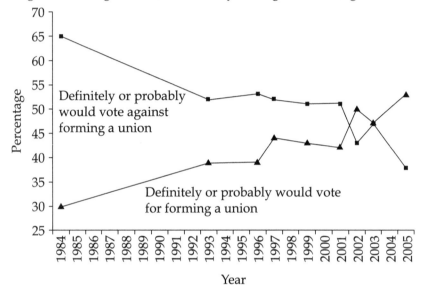

Source: Richard B. Freeman and Joel Rogers, exhibit I.6 *What Workers Want,*
2nd ed. (Ithaca; N.Y.: Cornell University Press, 2006.) Data from Hart Research Associates, various polls, except 1984; data for 1984 are from Harris, on a slightly differently worded question: "If an election were held tomorrow to decide whether your workplace would be unionized or not, do
you think you would definitely vote for a union, probably vote for a
union, probably vote against a union, or definitely vote against a union?"

Why Workers Want Unions

The workers who want unions want them to deal with workplace
problems that they believe management does not resolve ade-
quately or fairly. Figure 5.2 displays a measure of the number of

Figure 5.2   Number of Needs or Problems Workers Report at
             Their Workplace and the Proportion Who Say They
             Would Vote for a Union

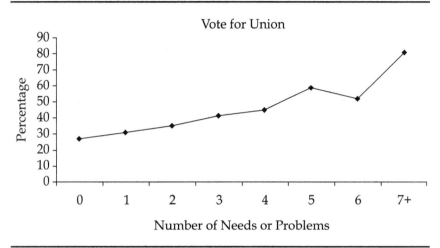

Vote for Union

Number of Needs or Problems

Source: Tabulated from Worker Representation and Participation Survey, available at: http://www.nber.org/~freeman/wrps.html.

needs or problems that non-union workers perceive at their workplace and the proportion of workers who would vote for a union in
a union representation election. The measure of needs or problems
is the sum across multiple items of the number of times workers
said there was a problem at their workplace or expressed a strong
desire for an improvement that management was not dealing with.
The desire for unionism is strongly related to the number of needs.
Among workers with no needs, 26 percent say that they would favor a union; among those with four needs, 45 percent say that they
would favor a union; among those with seven or more needs, 81
percent favor unions.

   The close tie between workers' desire for unionism and their perception that management is not taking care of workers can be seen
starkly in two questions that asked workers to grade management
on a standard A to F school mark. On a question about managerial
concern for workers, 71 percent of non-union workers who gave

management an F said that they would vote for the union, whereas barely one-third of workers who gave higher grades reported such a preference. On a question about management being *willing to share power* with workers, 69 percent of those who gave management an F grade said that they would vote for a union, compared to 47 percent who gave management a D grade, 35 percent who gave management a C grade, and just 20 percent who gave management an A or B grade.

In short, the workers who say that they want unions are responding to real problems at their workplace. They are not giving a quick, ill-informed "telephone answer to a hypothetical question."[16] Some undoubtedly reconsider their support for a union when management campaigns against a union or promises to remedy problems at the workplace without a union. But workers' desire for union representation is rooted in their workplace situation. A workplace with lots of problems produces lots of support for unions. A workplace with few problems produces little support for unions.

Consequences of the Decline in Unionism

Are American workers better or worse off with the declining rate of unionization than if unions had maintained their representation of the private sector at, say, the heady rates during the Reagan administration?

Studies from *What Do Unions Do?* through the mid-2000s show that unions raise the pay of workers, reduce inequality, increase pension coverage, provide health insurance, and give workers a democratic voice at their workplace. By bargaining for defined-benefit pension systems, unions create a way for workers to defer compensation into savings and provide for secure retirements. On the basis of these findings, we would expect declining union density to be associated with sluggish growth of real earnings for most workers, increased inequality, reductions in defined-benefit pensions, and more expensive and reduced health insurance. These are all areas in which workers have in fact lost ground. The decline of unions explains part of the declining economic position of U.S. workers, though it is by no means the main factor behind these changes.

Do unions raise or reduce productivity? To many economists, this is the $64 million question. Since anything that reduces productivity is prima facie bad, one of the major charges against unions has been that they reduce productivity. The evidence is clear: they do not. We know this with some certainty because researchers have used meta-statistical methods to collapse the results from a large number of studies into summary statistics. Meta-statistics is widely used in medical research to combine the results from small trials of medicines by doctors to give the appropriate statistical summary of all the studies taken together. In the union case, these analyses show that unions have slight positive impacts on productivity, but with wide variation among sectors.[17]

Going beyond productivity, studies find that unions reduce investments in capital and R&D and lower employment or employment growth in the organized sector. In the 1970s, some analysts argued that unions were partly responsible for some of the inflation of the period. The decline of unionism makes this discussion moot. If oil shocks or other factors induce a burst of inflation in the United States in the 2000s, no one will blame unions, since they no longer affect wage determination in the economy as a whole. On the other hand, the absence of a counterforce to management within firms has given management greater control over firms, so the decline of unionism should be associated with corporate excesses. Hello, Enron, AIG, Global Crossing . . .

Historically, unions used their political muscle to gain higher minimum wages, progressive taxes, and other legislation favorable to workers. As the union share of the workforce has fallen, so too has the union share of the electorate and union political influence, although much more slowly because so many of today's retirees worked during the heyday of unions.[18] Good-bye, national minimum-wage increases and strong legislation to control managerial excess.

Overall, is the economy better or worse off from the decline of unionism? If you are a worker below the top 10 percent of earners, you are worse off, having lost a force that operated on your behalf. If you are in the top 10 percent but below the top 1 percent or 0.1 percent, you probably are doing better than you would otherwise.

Ah, but if you are in the upper 1 percent or upper 0.1 percent, it could not get much better, though if you are a movie or recording star or a professional athlete, you would surely suffer if you lost your union.

The Future of Worker Representation

Workers in the United States want some form of collective voice in- side firms and in society. While unions have been the main institu- tional form for giving workers a say at their workplace in years past, perhaps some non-union form can substitute for unions in the future. Workers in other advanced countries where union member- ship is falling have not lost their say at the workplace, in part be- cause those countries permit or require firms to establish non- union institutions through which workers can express their collective interests to the firm. European countries mandate that firms set up works councils—elected committees of employees with specified rights—to meet and discuss workplace problems with management. Japan has a system of consultation and meet- ings with workers before management makes decisions. The An- glo-American countries whose institutions are closest to those of the United States—the United Kingdom, Australia, New Zealand, Ireland, and Canada—have staff associations, worker committees, and firm-sponsored non-union groups that provide representation and participation for employees.[19] Such non-union forms are illegal in the United States under section 8(a)(2) of the National Labor Re- lations Act, which outlaws company unions and has been legally interpreted to mean that any employer-supported group that dis- cusses worker issues is a company union. The employee involve- ment committees and quality circles and teams at U.S. workplaces focus on productivity and quality of output issues that improve profits; they cannot legally discuss improvements in wages and work conditions.

Some non-union organizations have tried to fill the gap in worker representation created by the decline of unions.[20] Public- interest legal organizations help workers in the enforcement of em- ployment laws, and human rights activists campaign for labor standards. But workers do not elect either of these types of groups, so they are not the voice of workers. Membership-based organizations such as the Industrial Areas Foundation, which organizes low-income communities to give voice to workers, and workers' centers for immigrants have the potential for representing the views of those they seek to aid.[21] The most comprehensive review of these non-union institutions concluded, however, that as of the early 2000s they had not developed the scale to substitute community-based voice for worker representation and participation in the labor market, nor were they likely to do so.[22]

Putting aside non-union alternatives, can traditional unionism resuscitate itself in the United States? Most experts believe that it cannot, which makes meetings on the future of unionism resemble wakes, even for researchers who do not particularly care for unions. (After all, the decline of unions means less interest in their work.) But unionism has been at the abyss before. In 1933, before the Depression-era growth in unionism, the president of the American Economic Association, George Barnett, declared that unions had no future. In the 1950s, just before unionism came to the public sector, George Meany declared that public-sector workers were non-organizable in the United States.

The problem with projecting the future of unions is that unions grow in discontinuous "spurts" in periods of social crisis, and nothing is more difficult to predict in the social sciences than discontinuous changes.[23] The social and economic factors associated with past union spurts do not produce easy generalization about what could bring about a future spurt. Union growth during World Wars I and II occurred during a tight wartime labor market that shifted the balance of power from business to workers and induced governments, which feared that industrial disputes would disrupt wartime production, to adopt policies that helped unions organize. Union growth during the Depression reflected a different dynamic: loss of faith in business leadership and economic desperation. The 1970s oil shock crisis led to union growth in Western Europe as workers sought protection against inflation through collective bargaining, but not in the United States, where the decline in private-sector unionism continued unabated. Perhaps U.S. division over the Vietnam War, which pitted many natural supporters of union-ism against the AFL-CIO, diverted activists from organizing in re-sponse to the oil-price-induced inflation.

Each of these spurts was associated with *changes in union form* that attracted groups of workers whom experts believed to be non-organizable or with *institutional or legal changes* that weakened em-ployer opposition. In the 1880s, the new form was the geographic lodge associated with the Knights of Labor. In the Depression, the new form was the industrial union. In World War II and earlier in World War I, labor boards and the compulsory arbitration of dis-putes over unionization compelled firms to accept them. The pub-lic-sector spurt transformed existing non-union associations, such as the National Education Association, into collective bargaining organizations. The associated legal change was the enactment of public-sector collective bargaining laws that forced public-sector employers to bargain collectively.

The lesson from labor history is that to recover from the endan-gered species list, unionism needs a new growth spurt associated with a new union form and new mode of operating.

Open-Source Unionism to the Rescue?

I have a solution to offer, based on the innovative ways in which some U.S. and U.K. unions have used the Internet and door-to-door canvassing to enlist new workers into labor activities. The so-lution is *open-source unionism*—a new union form that, like open-source programming, operates through networks rather than traditional bureaucracies. An open-source union enlists workers as members regardless of whether they can achieve majority-status unionism or collective contracts and, per its computer name, uses the Internet to connect those workers and deliver information and services to them at low cost. It brings workers together face to face in a geographic area rather than at an employer-dominated work-place. The Communication Workers of America, the United Auto-mobile Workers, the Machinists, and the Steelworkers, among others, have developed such forms.[24] But the most successful open-source innovation in the early 2000s was the AFL-CIO's non–collective bargaining "community affiliate to unionism": Working America.[25]

The AFL-CIO started Working America in the summer of 2004 by sending four hundred canvassers in ten cities to neighborhoods with many union members on the notion that residents there would have pro-union attitudes and thus be willing to join a union "affiliate."[26] Working America gathered the home addresses, telephone numbers, and email addresses of workers who wanted to join. The organization promised members that they would help determine policy through online ballots. The rate at which persons joined the organization stunned the federation: two-thirds of those canvassed signed up. Moreover, many had a political or social orientation that differed from that of most persons in the union movement: one-third were born-again Christians, 70 percent were conservatives or moderates in politics, and 32 percent supported the National Rifle Association (NRA). One-quarter of the members gave their email address, which allows Working America to communicate with them weekly. In 2005 and 2006, Working America spread its organizing drive to other cities in the country. As of this writing, Working America has two million members, which makes it the fastest-growing labor organization in U.S. history.

The key question that faces this new form is what it can do for its members outside of collective bargaining. Working America organizes campaigns on issues relevant to workers in their community. It encourages them to vote for candidates favorable to employees. It provides them with information. When the Bush administration changed the administrative rules governing overtime in August 2004, Working America added a page, "Is Your Overtime Pay at Risk?" to its website and hired a young lawyer to answer questions about the new ruling. As a result, Working America recruited over two thousand members per week via the Internet—a conversion rate of 7 percent of visitors to the site, about as high as any site can do.

The success of Working America validates the survey evidence that the United States has a vast untapped market for a labor organization to give voice to workers. Whether it or some comparable organization can develop a workplace presence or sufficient support services for workers to meet the unfilled demand for unionism is unclear. The split in the AFL-CIO may embolden the federation to pour more resources into Working America as its entry into the market for representation and participation. Or the split may lead the financially strapped federation to use Working America for political campaign purposes only.

Conclusion: What Next?

In sum, the decline in unionism in the United States has left most workers without an institution to represent their interests at the workplace. U.S. labor law does not allow firms to develop non-union initiatives like those in other advanced countries for fear that they will become bogus company-dominated organizations. At the same time, the law allows firms to effectively veto most efforts by unions to organize workers. The result is a massive and unprecedented unfilled demand for unionism. If unionism were a normal good or service, some smart organization or entrepreneur would step forward and find ways to meet the unfilled demand. Internet- and community-based open-source unions that operate outside of collective bargaining seem to offer the best chance for U.S. unions to expand membership and fill the massive representation and participation gap in the country.

❧ CHAPTER 6 ❧

REGULATING THE
UNREGULATED MARKET

- The boss walks into your office and yells, "You're fired!" Why? Because Donald Trump's television show inspired her. Legal or illegal?

- Management restructures the pension plan so that you get less and top management gets more. Legal or illegal?

- Your supervisor gives you one last assignment before sending your job to Bangalore: train your replacement. Legal or illegal?

- Changes at your workplace endanger safety. You protest. The firm fires you and hires temps to take your job. Legal or illegal?

Most Americans believe that unfair actions like these are illegal. The United States has the full panoply of labor regulations of an advanced economy. *Labor law* regulates wages and hours and other aspects of labor contracts and protects the right of workers to form unions and negotiate with employers collectively. *Employment law* outlaws discrimination on the basis of race, gender, ethnicity, religion, or disability. *Tax and spending policies* provide Social Security, disability insurance, unemployment insurance, and workers' compensation. In the 1970s and 1980s, Congress enacted laws on occupational health and safety, private pensions, and the employment of the disabled. Regulations protecting labor fill law texts and give employment to tens of thousands of lawyers.

Still, the U.S. regulatory system ranks at the bottom of the pack in protecting workers' rights at work and in ameliorating inequality in labor market outcomes. The United States operates under an *employment at will* doctrine in which the firm owns the job. This means that it is legal for your boss to fire you because Trump inspired her, to change its benefit plan in ways that harm you, to order you to train your replacement, and to fire you for protesting dangers at the workplace. The United States has few inspectors or regulators administering wage and hours legislation or occupational health and safety regulations. It lacks the works councils that the European Union uses to protect rights at workplaces or the "internal responsibility" committees that Canada uses to help enforce labor laws. The exceptional way for U.S. workers to enforce their rights is through court proceedings. You think the firm has violated your legal rights? Get a lawyer and sue. Will your lawsuit succeed? A lawsuit or the threat of a suit can work to enforce the law in some situations. In other situations, it burdens employers but does little to help workers.

The Success of Equal Employment

One great success of the United States in regulating the labor market is in equal employment. Before Title VII of the 1964 Civil Rights Act outlawed employment discrimination in the job market, some states had equal employment acts that penalized discrimination, but most blacks lived in the southern states, where discrimination was the norm. Firms advertised jobs for whites or men only, refused to hire blacks or women for some jobs, or promoted white men over better-qualified workers from other groups without any legal consequences. Few corporate recruiters visited the historically black colleges and universities where most black students studied. As a result, black college graduates taught in segregated schools or provided professional services in the black community or worked for the government. The earnings of blacks were about 60 percent of those of whites, a ratio comparable to what it was in Reconstruction days.

The Civil Rights Act was initially designed to outlaw discrimination against blacks, but a southern congressman opposed to the bill insisted that women be covered as well. The inclusion of women was meant to mock the bill since women's "natural place" was in the home and discriminating against them in the job market was part of the natural order of economic life. The Civil Rights Act was followed by President Johnson's Executive Order 11246 (1969), which required firms with federal contracts to take "affirmative action" to remedy the low numbers of persons in protected groups whom they employed.

Analysts and policymakers did not expect the act to have an immediate effect on the economic position of blacks, but the earnings and occupational attainment of black workers did begin rising relative to those of white workers from the mid-1960s through the early 1970s. The number of national corporate recruiters interviewing on black college campuses jumped. Realizing that they could get jobs in the large firms, black students shifted their majors from education and social service to business administration and other fields associated with business. I wrote some of my earliest papers about the "good news" that the law had worked in breaking the barrier of discrimination.[1] I thought the outside world was going to be as convinced by the new analysis as I had been when I was poring over the statistics on black economic progress.

The papers attracted attention but also received a barrage of criticism. Many scholars were unconvinced that the anti-bias laws and policies were effective. Civil rights advocates worried that the evidence that blacks were doing better would lead the government to weaken the civil rights law or its enforcement. Some analysts argued that the late 1960s Vietnam War boom was the real factor behind the strong job market for blacks. The last time blacks had advanced relative to whites in the economy was during the tight labor market of World War II. This explanation bit the dust when blacks held on to their gains in the recession of the mid-1970s. Other analysts argued that the gains that blacks made were temporary because blacks were taking jobs with high current salaries while whites were investing in jobs with low starting salaries but greater gains in earnings over time. Yet others suggested that government welfare programs were inducing blacks to leave the job market, which drove up their wages. Conservatives were troubled by the possibility that affirmative action, which smacked of quotas in employment, might be driving black economic gains and argued that affirmative action's temporary benefits would hurt blacks over time. All of these alternatives also bit the dust as time went on, and a broad consensus emerged that while the equal employment legislation did not eliminate the historic disadvantages that had impoverished the black community, it successfully supplanted blatant discrimination in the job market with pressures for affirmative action.

Why did the equal employment and affirmative action policies work? It was not because the Equal Employment Opportunity Commission, the agency that monitored Title VII, penalized miscreant firms to any significant degree. Nor was it because affirmative action imposed the quotas that conservatives feared. Rather, the anti-bias policies were effective for two reasons: because class-action court suits threatened firms with sizable penalties and bad publicity that outweighed any benefits from maintaining discrimination; and because management in large firms found that increasing the diversity of the workforce had no deleterious effect on company performance and thus came to see that doing "what was right" made good business sense. By making the meeting of equal employment goals a criterion in promoting managers and supervisors, firms induced their middle managers and supervisors to take the company affirmative action goals seriously.

Although the court system of enforcing antidiscrimination law worked, going to court to defend your rights is not for everyone. In the mid-1980s, the hospital where my sister worked decided to reduce its medical staff by laying off young female MDs while keeping on male MDs near retirement. The women were outraged at this blatant discrimination. What could they do? I asked the chief lawyer at the AFL-CIO for his advice and was surprised when he recommended that the women should forget the law and get other jobs. As doctors, they could easily find high-paying jobs elsewhere. If they brought a discrimination suit forward, other hospitals might be leery of hiring them, their case could go on for several years, and their legal expenses would be high. My sister and the other female MDs chose to find jobs elsewhere. Two years later, the hospital brought my sister back as head of her department. The market worked. Perhaps the legal system would have worked as well, but perhaps not.

Good Intentions Are Not Enough

About one in ten persons in every society suffer from some physical, mental, or psychological disability that impairs their ability to work productively.[2] About 2 percent of persons are sufficiently disabled that they cannot make a living at a regular job. Society or their families must supplement their earnings. The Americans with Disability Act (ADA), which is the main U.S. legislation to help disabled workers navigate the labor market, neither supplements earnings nor covers the costs of hiring less productive disabled persons. Instead, it requires employers with fifteen or more employees "to make reasonable accommodation to the known physical or mental limitations of otherwise qualified individuals with disabilities, unless it results in undue hardship."[3] If you believe an employer has not made reasonable accommodation for your disability and could do so with no undue hardship, the law enables you to take your case to the EEOC and to court. In 2005, 20 percent of all charges brought to EEOC were about employer treatment of the disabled.[4]

Advanced European countries and Japan protect their disabled workers in a different way. They require that firms hire a certain percentage of disabled workers at the *going wage rate* for their job (which is easiest to do when institutions determine wages), and they tax those firms for which such hires would be an undue hardship and use the money to subsidize those that hire the disabled. Thus, the disabled earn normal wages even when they are less productive than other workers while society recompenses their employer for the gap between wages and productivity.

Which works better in helping the disabled navigate the job market—lawsuits or quotas with taxes and subsidies? Quotas with taxes and subsidies. The proportion of the disabled who are employed is higher in advanced Europe and Japan than in the United States, and the income of the disabled is closer to that of the able-bodied in these countries than in the United States.[5] In addition, looking solely within the United States, enactment of the ADA did not improve the economic position of the average disabled person.

Employment of the disabled relative to the able-bodied either fell or remained constant after the act, while the relative earnings of the disabled actually fell.[6]

When the Right Is Right: Welfare Reform

[An] outrage . . . that will hurt and impoverish millions of American children.
—Marian Wright Edelman, president, Children's Defense Fund[7]

At a time when most married mothers with young children stayed at home to take care of the children, the United States developed Aid to Families with Dependent Children (AFDC) to provide income support for single mothers so that they could do the same. AFDC support was never high enough to allow welfare mothers to stay home without some other income. California was one of the most generous states in the heyday of AFDC, in part owing to a welfare reform bill signed by Governor Ronald Reagan. In 1977 the state paid $302 per family in current dollars (nearly $1,000 in 2005 dollars). By contrast, Mississippi, the lowest-income southern state, paid just $47 per month per family in current dollars; other southern states also paid relatively little.[8] The combination of AFDC and food stamps left most single-parent families far below the poverty line. Most single mothers earned extra money under the table from work or received income from the missing fathers or other relatives that they did not report to the government.

Conservatives disliked the AFDC program because it gave the wrong incentives to low-income families. It discouraged lower-income men from staying with their children and discouraged single mothers from working, as Charles Murray made vivid in his 1984 book on welfare, *Losing Ground*.[9] When more married women with young children began to choose to work in the 1980s and 1990s, the idea that the government should support single mothers who were not working lost attractiveness. If the goal of policy was to make single-parent families more like two-parent families, shouldn't the government be encouraging single mothers to work rather than paying them not to work?

In 1996, following the Republican triumph in the 1994 elections, Congress and President Bill Clinton replaced "welfare as we know it" with the program Temporary Assistance for Needy Families (TANF), which allowed welfare recipients to receive benefits for at most two continuous years and for no more than five years over their lifetime. In addition, the welfare reform legislation, the Personal Responsibility and Work Opportunity Reconciliation Act (PRWORA), insisted that states have 80 percent of their welfare clients working or searching for work within a few years. Since no one was sure what policies might accomplish this—child care, training, job search assistance—Congress gave the states block grants to spend on helping welfare mothers transition into work as they saw fit.

As the quotation from Marian Wright Edelman indicates, most liberals opposed the act. The program was risky. If the economy tanked and there were no jobs for the welfare mothers, what would happen to them and their children? Many welfare mothers had such limited skills that they could never earn enough to provide for their families even if they found a job. And the sudden entry of tens of thousands of welfare recipients into local job markets threatened to depress earnings for low-wage workers and add to unemployment.

In the case of welfare reform, however, the right had it right. Welfare mothers found jobs in the booming economy of the 1990s and continued to work in the weaker job market that followed. The number of welfare recipients plummeted from 12.2 million in August 1996 to 4.5 million in June 2005.[10] The labor participation rate of single mothers with children younger than five years of age increased by twenty percentage points. Upwards of two-thirds of persons leaving welfare found employment, albeit at low wages that left most of them below the poverty line.[11] Welfare reform succeeded in getting women who had seemed to be permanently dependent on welfare into the world of work. It succeeded because welfare mothers respond to incentives. It did not succeed in reducing the poverty rate among single-parent families because wages are low on the lower rungs of the earnings distribution.

When the Left Is Right: Making Work Pay

There are two ways to raise the earnings of low-wage workers: increase their pay with a minimum wage or supplement their pay through negative income taxes or provision of free goods or services. Since 1935, the United States has had a minimum wage. In 2005 between two and three million workers were paid minimum or near-minimum wages.[12] Since 1975, the United States has used the Earned Income Tax Credit (EITC) to supplement the incomes of lower-income families. In 2003, 22.1 million families received EITC payments that averaged $2,100 (and more for lower-income families).[13]

The minimum wage is a contentious policy because higher wages can reduce employment, so that an ill-chosen minimum wage may cause more harm through job loss than good through higher pay. To assess the minimum wage as a redistributive tool we must determine how many jobs the minimum wage costs society. A minimum wage that doubles the pay of, say, 500,000 low-wage workers at the cost of 100 jobs would be a highly efficient tool for improving their earnings. If the same minimum wage cost 100,000 jobs, it would be a much less efficient tool. Studies in the 1960s and 1970s suggested that changes in the minimum wage had modest adverse effects on employment: a 10 percent increase in the minimum wage would reduce employment by about 1 percent.[14] This meant that the share of income going to the low-paid would rise with an increase in the minimum wage. But critics noted that some of that shift in income went to teenagers or others in high-income families rather than to the poor.

The debate over the minimum wage heated up in the 1990s and 2000s when David Card and Alan Krueger found that employment did not decline in states that increased their minimum wage compared to those that did not, even among workers in low-wage industries where the minimum wage had a significant bite.[15] No effect of the minimum wage on employment? Some economists viewed this finding as heresy—a denial that the demand curve for labor slopes down. But economics tells a more complicated story about the minimum wage than that it invariably reduces employment. When a firm hires all the labor it wants at a constant wage, increasing that wage should reduce employment, but when a firm faces an upward-sloping supply of labor, an increase in the minimum can raise employment.[16] Even in that case, however, if government were to set a minimum wage high enough—say, by adding a zero after the current level—employment would certainly contract massively. With an unrealistically high minimum wage, firms would not have the revenues to pay their workers. The policy question is not about whether demand curves slope downward at high levels of the minimum wage, but about how firms respond to modest changes in modest levels of the minimum wage. In the real world, no government wants to raise minimum wages to the levels that cause substantial job losses. When the United Kingdom introduced its minimum wage in the 1990s, the policy discussion was about the level at which employers would find other ways to adjust to the higher cost than about displacing workers.

When the federal government allowed the minimum wage to fall in real terms from 1996 to 2006, many states raised their minimum wages and many cities introduced "living wages"—minimum wages focused on particular employers, often city contractors. These increases in wages did not affect employment to any noticeable extent. State- or city-level minimum wages tailored to the specific economic conditions of an area or employer are less likely to have deleterious effects on employment than a single national minimum wage that imposes the same rate on high-wage Connecticut as on low-wage Mississippi.

The EITC is a negative income tax for workers that many economists from Milton Friedman on the right to James Tobin on the left have favored as the most direct way to aid the working poor. Unlike the minimum wage, the EITC does not cost jobs. The first order effect of EITC makes work more attractive—for example, the household that earned $14,000 in 2006 got $2,747 from Uncle Sam if it had one child, and $4,536 if it had two children.[17] That effect should increase the supply of workers.[18] By the 1990s and 2000s, however, the politics had changed. Liberals supported the EITC, but conservatives now favored huge tax cuts to the super-wealthy as the best economic policy for the country.

The EITC is imperfect. It creates niches with very high implicit tax rates on workers who work more hours or obtain higher wages.

This happens because they lose some of their EITC tax rebate when their income rises. At the same time, by inducing more persons to enter the workforce, the EITC reduces the wage for low-wage workers. Even with these flaws, however, the EITC has been effective in shifting income toward the lower-paid. The Clinton administration's 1993 increase in the EITC improved the income of more workers by a greater amount than the administration's increase in the minimum wage. Indicative of the success of the EITC, other countries have also adopted negative income taxes to raise the income of low-wage workers.

Finally, while Congress considers minimum wages and the EITC separately, the economics of transferring income to the poor suggests that the two policies complement one another. The minimum wage offsets the decline in wages that might occur from an EITC-induced increase in supply. The EITC directs income gains toward low-income families rather than low-wage teens. Together, the minimum wage and the EITC share the cost of raising the income of the low-paid between purchasers of their goods and services and taxpayers.

When the Aged Are Right: Pensions and Social Security

Social Security is the most successful income support program in the United States. It has enabled the country to reduce poverty massively among the elderly. By pooling huge sums of money, Social Security has low administrative expenses: just 0.7 percent of its outlays go for administrative cost annually. This compares to costs of 2 to 3 percent per year for financial firms to run individual investment accounts.[19] By guaranteeing fixed retirement benefits, moreover, Social Security moves the risk of funding retirement from workers or firms to the federal government, which is better able to absorb risk.

Still, every decade or so we are told that Social Security is going bankrupt and must be changed. In 1983 the Greenspan Commission warned that the Social Security fund would run out in 2015. In the mid-1990s, the Advisory Council Commission on Social Security reported that the fund would be unable to pay full benefits in 2030. A decade later, however, the date at which the fund would be depleted was set at 2042. The Bush administration called for partial privatization of the fund, with some moneys placed in individual accounts that could be invested in the stock market.[20] What fuels these concerns is that Social Security is a pay-as-you-go system in which the taxes of current workers pay the pensions of current retirees. Its solvency depends on the number of workers (and their wages) relative to the number of retirees (and their Social Security pensions). When the number of workers falls relative to the number of retirees, which will happen when the baby boomers retire, the government has to rebalance the system. It can raise taxes on workers or reduce benefits for retirees. Reducing benefits can take the form of lowering the amount that recipients get or extending the retirement age at which persons normally receive the funds.

Given this choice, might the country do better to "privatize" Social Security? Privatization shifts responsibility for Social Security from a government-guaranteed payment to workers, who place funds into legally required individual retirement accounts. If your private account does well, you have higher retirement earnings. If your private account does poorly, well . . . that's the way it goes. The main argument for privatization is that people could invest their money in the stock market, where rewards average 7 percent over the long run—far above the 3 to 4 percent that Social Security obtains from Treasury notes or the growth of tax receipts, which roughly parallels the growth of GDP. The higher average returns from private investment accounts would make the average person better off. If the flow of funds into the stock market induced firms to invest more, the growth rate of the economy would increase, creating a bigger pie to share among retirees and workers.

The privatization story sounds good at first blush, but you do not raise your return in any investment from 3 to 4 percent to 7 percent without paying a cost. The 7 percent return on the stock market exceeds the 4 percent on Treasury notes because the stock market is riskier. If we knew for certain that we could get 7 percent by holding shares, no one would buy Treasury notes. But there is no certainty in the stock market, as many investors and pension funds learned to their chagrin with the collapse of the dot-com boom in the 2000s. Since many investors make financially foolish decisions—holding far too much of their assets in the stocks of their employer or trading shares too often—the risks of individual blunders compound the risks of market fluctuations. In addition, as noted, individual accounts cost more to administer. Indeed, it is the high servicing charges that make Wall Street firms salivate at the thought of privatization, since much of the possible higher returns would go to financial firms rather than to retirees. Finally, the shift from tax-funded Social Security to mandated private accounts creates a transition problem: one generation must pay Social Security taxes while also saving in their individual accounts for themselves.[21]

These problems do not mean that investing part of Social Security funds in shares is a horrific idea. Some countries have created successful individual accounts for retirement savings on top of their equivalent of Social Security. Sweden added a 3 percent tax on top of its normal social security arrangements for workers to invest in pension funds subject to a maximum management fee. Australia developed a successful, government-mandated "super-annuation" (pension) system of individual accounts. Switzerland has secured retirement incomes through private accounts, with the funds invested largely in safe securities rather than in shares.[22] Britain's effort to move workers into private occupational pension systems, however, ended in disaster. Financial groups sold workers investments that reduced rather than raised their potential retirement incomes. Private firms found that the risks of funding pension plans for workers were so great that they closed the funds to new employees or dropped their private schemes altogether. As a result, the U.K. pensions and retirement system has been in crisis.[23]

The U.S. private retirement system also has problems. Some private pension funds are underfunded. Their trustees thought their funds were doing fine in the 1990s stock market boom and allowed the firms to contribute less while they increased the level of pensions. Some funds are in trouble because the trustees and actuaries failed to take adequate account of the risks of holding large proportions of pension assets in shares.[24] The federal government's Pension Benefit Guaranty Corporation (PBGC), which monitors and insures defined-benefit private pension plans, has struggled to deal with bankruptcies in the steel and airline industries. If large pension funds run by big corporations can get their investments so wrong, imagine the problems that might afflict ordinary workers. In 2006 the Congressional Budget Office (CBO) estimated that privatization of Social Security in the United States had a sizable chance of creating financial problems for retirees compared to Social Security. To provide pensioners with the same retirement incomes they would get under Social Security would require a huge federal expenditure.[25] Making modest adjustments in retirement age and in Social Security taxes seems a safer way to respond to the retirement of baby boomers than devising a new private accounts system that would place every person on their own investment boat in the turbulent ocean of financial markets.[26]

How Much Redistribution?

Income distributions are invariably unequal and skewed. For every Bill Gates, there are tens of thousands of lower-paid Bills. In a democracy, where every citizen has one vote, government policies should favor the lower-paid Bills and offset some of the inequality that the market produces. In fact, that is what policymakers invariably do. Democratic governments (and many nondemocratic governments as well) tend to redistribute income to the poorer parts of society. This practice is so widespread as to constitute what I call the third law of earnings dispersion: *the state uses its tax and spend policies to reduce the dispersion of income.*[27]

But here too the United States is exceptional. The United States does less redistribution through tax and benefit programs than other countries. Figure 6.1 documents this by comparing the pre– and post–tax and transfer Gini coefficient measures of inequality of the United States and three groups of countries: the Nordic countries, which have extensive welfare states; other OECD countries such as Germany and France; and the English-speaking countries of Canada, Australia, and the United Kingdom. The United States starts off with the highest measure of inequality and ends up with the highest measure of inequality. Each country's tax and transfer policies reduce inequality. The reduction is smaller for the United States than for the comparison groups.[28] The figure does not identify the full or true ef-

Figure 6.1   Gini Coefficient Measures of Inequality in the
             United States and Other Advanced Countries,
             Pre–Tax and Transfer and Post–Tax and Transfer,
             1970s to 1990s

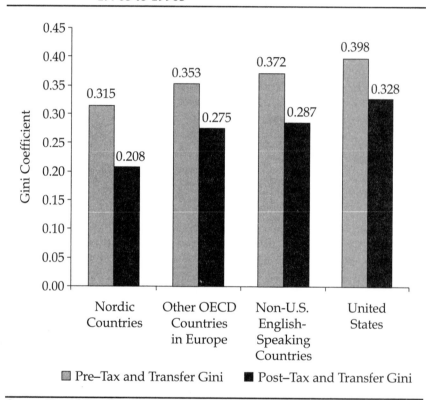

■ Pre–Tax and Transfer Gini   ■ Post–Tax and Transfer Gini

Source: David Bradley, Evelyne Huber, Stephanie Moller, François Nielsen, and John D. Stephens, "Distribution and Redistribution in Postindustrial Democracies," *World Politics* 55 (2, January 2003): 193–228, table 2.
Note: The Nordic countries are Sweden, Norway, Denmark, and Finland. The other OECD countries in Europe are Belgium, the Netherlands, Germany, France, Italy, and Switzerland. The non-U.S. English-speaking countries are Canada, Australia, and the United Kingdom. Reprinted with permission from The Johns Hopkins University Press.

fect of government policies, since the figures in the pre–tax and transfer column already reflect some policies and responses to those policies. For instance, providing high benefits to low-wage workers through tax relief may decrease the incomes of these workers in the before column, since they will have an incentive to work less to obtain the benefits. Still, the pattern is clear, and it can be found in the differing benefits associated with the major programs that provide a social insurance safety net in the United States and in other countries: unemployment benefits, sickness leave, and welfare support to poor families are lower in the United States than elsewhere.

But the most striking difference is in the provision of health insurance, which Americans obtain through their employers rather than as citizens. The U.S. health care system takes up 13 percent of GDP, employs 20 million workers, and is arguably the least efficient part of the U.S. economy—a drag on productivity and economic well-being. The United States spends nearly twice as much of GDP on health care as the average advanced OECD country without getting any better health outcomes.[29] This is something to be fixed.

The response of the United States to the increase in income inequality from the 1980s to the 2000s highlights the exceptional way in which the United States responds to inequality. When inequality began to rise in the late 1970s and early 1980s, I expected that both political parties would seek to lean against the wind of market forces and choose tax and spending policies that favored the average citizen or those in the lower parts of the income distribution. The Democrats would seek to raise the minimum wage while the Republicans would use the EITC to augment the family incomes of the low-paid. This is not what happened. The Reagan tax cut did more for the rich than for the rest of society. Bush senior also cut taxes for the rich. The Clinton administration did the same, though it also increased the EITC. Blessed with the huge unexpected surplus in the federal budget in 1999–2000, the administration of Bush junior showed its compassionate conservative philosophy by compassionately enacting an even larger tax cut for the rich.

I complained about the 2002 Bush tax cut to my conservative friends. I favored using the unexpected surplus to give a temporary lump sum payment to every citizen, as Alaska does with its royalties from the state's oil funds—a policy supported by Republicans, Democrats, liberals, and conservatives in the state.[30] I opposed the tax plan of cutting checks to the super-wealthy as income redistribution from those in need to those without need. My friends answered that there was a moral logic for giving the tax cuts to the rich. It was their money. The government had taken it from them and was obligated to give it back whenever it could. I disagree. Citizens earn their money under a set of social rules that include those of the tax system. When the tax take is larger than expected, the moral principle should be to cut the taxes to those in greatest need, not to those in least need. Alternatively, the government ought to invest money in areas that improve the economy—infrastructure, R&D, scholarships for education—or put it toward reducing the national debt. I understand why someone in the upper 10 percent . . . er, 1 percent . . . er, 0.1 percent . . . might favor policies that create more inequality. It is economic greed, which economists study ad infinitum. But morality? Not in any religion I know of.

Conclusion

The United States is exceptional in the way it regulates the labor market and the outcomes the market generates. The United States relies extensively on court suits to protect workers from discrimination and other illegal employer acts, with disparate effects on workers. Suing in court works for some groups of workers but not for others, so U.S. labor regulations do less to reduce disparities in the way the labor market treats workers than the regulatory procedures in other countries. In addition, the United States does less to redistribute income from the super-rich to poorer citizens. As inequality increased in the last two decades of the twentieth century through the mid-2000s, Republican administrations abandoned their historic commitment to the Earned Income Tax Credit in favor of tax policies that benefited the super-rich. As Robert Dole once said about a somewhat different matter, where is the outrage over this? Where is the conservative outrage about policies that enrich those with plenty at the expense of the majority of citizens?

❧ CHAPTER 7 ❧

MANAGEMENT IN THE DRIVER'S SEAT

We are in a market economy for hourly labor to make components for automobiles . . . and we are well under market with
what we pay the senior leadership team.
—Steve Miller, CEO, Delphi Corporation, announcing that the
firm would ask for 60 percent pay cuts, elimination of retiree
benefits, and the closing of most of its forty-four U.S. plants,
while asking bankruptcy courts to approve bonuses for hundreds of executives[1]

With unions in abeyance and weakly enforced government regulations, management determines what happens at most
workplaces. The well-being of workers depends on how management organizes work, deals with problems at the workplace, and
divides revenues among workers, shareholders, and managers.

The "invisible hand" model gives management little independent say in how it treats workers or in other critical business decisions. Your boss's behavior, be it wonderful or horrid, reflects market conditions. If the market for people is tight and you can readily
leave for a new job, your boss will either treat you well or pay you
a lot for the abuse you take. Conversely, if the firm can make more
money treating you badly, your boss had better be tough on you. To
paraphrase the comedian Flip Wilson's famous line "The Devil
made me do it," in this vision of economic life management is never
responsible for what it does: "The Market made them do it."[2]

Managers have a different view. They believe that they have
greater discretion in decisions than the invisible hand model envi-
sions. Why would firms pay managers high salaries if they simply
did what the market said? Why earn the MBA if markets speak
clearly and all you have to do is listen and go with the flow? Econ-

omists use principal-agent models to analyze management independence. These models focus on the need for shareholders (the principal) to give incentives to management (the agent) to behave in the interests of the firm. For instance, awarding stock options or shares to top executives is designed to align their interests with those of shareholders. But the model also speaks to the ways in which management (now the principal) treats workers (the agents) to align their interests with those of the firm.

Whether management discretion departs from or reflects the invisible hand, the American job market generates huge differences in working conditions and in the treatment of workers across firms. The star actors and actresses, who have outside market opportunities, are treated better than the bit players, who do not have such opportunities, and the stars are also paid much more.

Human Resource Management Policies

Most large firms have departments of human resource management to deal with employees and employee problems. When unions were strong and firms dealt with workers collectively, these departments specialized in *industrial relations* and set *personnel policy*, a term that signaled concern with the psychological well-being of employees. Some large firms developed employee assistance programs (EAPs) to help workers recover from alcohol, drug, or psychological problems that impaired their productivity instead of doing what would have come naturally—firing them.[3] The term "human resource management" implies a more hardheaded economic approach to managing employees; from this perspective, management sees workers as a "resource," like machines or materials, in the production process.

This hardheaded perspective came to the fore in October 2005 when the *New York Times* described an internal Wal-Mart memorandum that outlined how top executives were thinking about ways to cut the costs of employee benefits while avoiding bad publicity and employee backlash. One of the policies under consideration was to order all "associates" (Wal-Mart's lingo for "workers") to engage in physical activity such as gathering carts. The firm hoped that this would discourage unhealthy persons from applying for jobs, which would reduce the costs associated with sickness. Since federal law requires firms to accommodate the physical or mental limitations of disabled employees unless doing so would cause undue hardship to the firm, the proposed policy was probably illegal. The memo also suggested that the firm reduce contributions to 401(k) pension plans and to its employee life insurance program. The memo was forthright in recognizing that "Wal-Mart's critics are correct in some of their observations regarding expensive health care insurance and the dependence of many employees and their children on public assistance," but it did not propose ways to reduce the costs to employees of health insurance or their dependence on public assistance. Instead, the memo expressed concern about employees who remained with the firm for long periods and earned seniority pay but were no more productive than new hires and about full-time workers who worked less than forty hours a week while qualifying for health and other benefits. As described in the news reports about the memo, Wal-Mart fit the picture that community and labor activists had painted of the nation's leading retailer as the archetypical bad employer seeking to squeeze its employees as much as possible.

When I downloaded and read the memo, I was neither surprised nor unnerved by Wal-Mart's analysis of its employee benefits.[4] The memo made good economic sense. Management wanted to reduce the costs of benefits without upsetting employees and without creating more bad publicity for its labor practices. It considered how different cuts in benefits would affect costs, the job satisfaction of employees, and public scrutiny. There was no morality in its assessment of these factors, just concern about making profits. It would have been worth an A in any human resource management course.

In fact, despite all the criticism directed at Wal-Mart, the firm is not a bad employer. It has done some bad things but, on the American spectrum, nothing so egregious as to make it the bogeyman of the labor market. Wal-Mart has been in court for allegedly illegally using undocumented workers; failing to give California workers legally required meal and rest benefits; and violating Fair Labor Standards Act rules on hours worked and overtime pay. Wal-Mart

111

has closed facilities when workers voted to unionize in North America while working with China's state run unions to "organize" Wal-Mart workplaces there. While Wal-Mart pays less and offers lower benefits than some of its competitors, such as Costco, its compensation package suffices to recruit workers in the low-wage locales where it locates stores.

What draws the ire of the labor and community activists who attack Wal-Mart is that with the economic power and profits that accrue from being the world's leading retailer, Wal-Mart could be a much better employer than it is. It could raise pay and benefits considerably without doing much damage to its bottom line or market share.[5] It could set a high standard for compensating lower-skilled Americans. Instead, Wal-Mart has chosen to get by with what the market allows. The market did not dictate that choice. Management made the decision following cold calculations like those shown in the memo. Seemingly following its strategy of squeezing out higher-paid senior employees, Wal-Mart has raised the share of its workers who are part-time, and it demands that senior employees be available to work anytime; the company controls the scheduling of work regardless of its employees' situations.[6]

This human resource management strategy has costs, which at some time might lead Wal-Mart to reconsider it. With its huge turnover—about half of Wal-Mart's employees leave in a year—the company has very high recruitment and training costs. But if long-term employees are no more productive than new hires, why should Wal-Mart worry about turnover? Wal-Mart's labor policies make it a target for unions and community activists, who have sought state laws and city ordinances to force the firm to increase spending on health benefits. But if Wal-Mart can fend off these activists at lower cost than raising its compensation, why give more to workers and less to management and shareholders? And having many employees and their children on public assistance simply means that taxpayers are funding some of the cost of Wal-Mart's labor, which is also good for profits.

In the 1990s, another leading firm, Nike, was the butt of criticism from labor and human rights activists, in this case because of poor working conditions in the factories in the developing countries where Nike manufactured its sneakers. The anti-sweatshop movement blamed Nike for failing to make its overseas subcontractors treat employees decently and live up to Nike's own corporate code of conduct. The firm's huge factory in Indonesia, which produced a large share of its sneakers, had abysmal health and safety standards. For several years, Nike battled the critics. It refused to disclose the location of its subcontractors on the grounds that this was a competitive secret. It refused to have independent observers monitor its facilities. It refused to improve health and safety conditions because that was too expensive. But by the 2000s what proved too expensive was fighting the critics. Whenever the human rights campaign against Nike heated up, the firm's price fell on the stock market. There was a continual risk that charges of poor labor practices would sully the firm's reputation enough that it would lose customers. Nike got its act together and became a leader in improving labor conditions overseas. Nike did this not because its top leadership decided to sacrifice profits for the good of workers, but because the firm realized that it could secure its profitability more by trying to improve labor standards than by fighting the human rights and labor activists.[7]

The lesson for those who want Wal-Mart and other large and profitable employers to do better by their workers is that the road to better behavior is paved with viable threats to profits. At this writing, the Chicago city council has passed a "retail living wage ordinance" to force Wal-Mart and other large retailers to pay a minimum wage of $10 per hour and $3 per hour in health insurance. Wal-Mart has threatened to suspend its planned store openings in the city and managed to get the mayor of Chicago to veto the ordinance and the city council to uphold the veto. But the proponents of the bill will undoubtedly come back next year . . . and the year after. If Wal-Mart can make good money paying higher wages and benefits, the economist in me predicts that Wal-Mart will eventually open in Chicago as a better employer. If the other large retailers can pay higher wages and benefits and remain profitable, surely the most efficient retailer of them all can do so also.

What Firms Do

Managements that choose a positive human resources strategy use a diverse set of policies and practices to resolve the problems that invariably arise between employers and employees at workplaces.

The most common practice, an "open-door" policy, covers half of the workforce in larger workplaces and allows workers to bring any problem to managers higher than their supervisor at almost any time. Open-door systems usually deal with the problems that affect individuals, but some companies also have open doors for groups of workers. When I first heard management talk about open-door policies, I thought they were Mickey Mouse nonsense: you go to the top manager, you gripe, the manager says something, and the firm does little. But workers in firms with open-door policies for group issues report 30 percent fewer workplace problems than firms without such policies. And workers in non-union firms with open-door policies report higher levels of job satisfaction and less desire for a union than other workers.[8] So these policies have an effect.

Large firms have other policies to connect with workers. Many firms hold regular town meetings that resemble the assemblies held in elementary or secondary schools. Many conduct employee attitude surveys regularly. Many rely extensively on employee involvement committees or teams to make production decisions on their own. On the Workplace Representation and Participation Survey that Joel Rogers and I conducted in the mid-1990s, half of the workers reported that their firm had an employee involvement program, and nearly one-third said that they participated in the program. Workers on these committees had fewer problems at their workplace and were less likely to want a union than other workers. What are less common in the United States are committees of employees who discuss *labor issues* with management on a *regular* basis. But even this relatively uncommon practice covers more workers than do trade unions.[9]

To what extent, if at all, do these and other human resource management practices make U.S. firms "good employers"?

The WRPS asked workers about problems at work in ten different areas. The number of times they reported a problem or said they wanted something to change provides a metric for assessing how well U.S. employers do. Workers whose employer treats them well should report few problems. Workers whose employer treats them poorly should report many problems. The largest number of workers—about 40 percent—reported no problems at their workplace. Thus, a substantial number of firms were very good indeed. Most other workers reported a few problems. But a small number of workers reported many problems at their workplace. These tended to be laborers or semiskilled workers, those employed in manufacturing or mining or wholesale trade, black workers, or older workers. But irrespective of the characteristics of the worker, the industry, or the occupation, the most important factor determining workplace problems was the particular workplace itself. When one worker at a location reported problems, other workers at that location were also likely to report problems.[10] This means that problems were endemic to that workplace and to the way management operated there. This is true even across workplaces in the same firm operating under the same company rules. At some Citicorp branches in New York, many workers were dissatisfied with their workplace, while at seemingly equivalent branches workers were satisfied.[11] Workplace human relations are a local phenomenon.

Finally, the WRPS asked workers to grade management in various areas using school grades A to F. Most workers gave management A and B scores in knowledge of the business. But many fewer gave management high scores in employee relations. In sharing power with workers, 13 percent gave management an A grade compared to 24 percent who gave them D or F grades. In giving fair pay increases, 18 percent gave management an A grade compared to 21 percent who gave them D or F grades. Workers rated management a bit better in "concern for employees": 23 percent gave them an A versus 17 percent who gave them a D or F, but the overall picture is a dismal one.[12]

Alternative Dispute Resolution

You have just had a terrible day at work. Your supervisor treated you horribly, possibly breaking employment or labor law or the company's handbook of rules for personnel issues. But you don't want to sue in court, and you don't want to quit the job. Is there anything you can do to alleviate your problem? In union settings, workers can raise a grievance about how the firm treated them and carry the grievance to a neutral arbitrator for a final decision. This is faster, cheaper, and better than court suits because labor arbitrators know more about labor practices than judges. In 1960 the Supreme Court declared grievance arbitration to be a preferred dispute resolution technique and told the lower courts that they could not overturn arbitrators' awards unless the arbitrator did something blatantly egregious.[13]

In the 1980s and 1990s, some large non-union firms sought to develop a non-union equivalent to the grievance arbitration system. To enable their workers to resolve workplace disputes without expensive court suits, they established alternative dispute resolution (ADR) systems, which allowed workers to bring a problem at company expense to an outside arbitrator, who could overturn management's decision. In the union setting, the union and firm shared the cost of the arbitrator, and each could usually veto an arbitrator whom they regarded as biased, so the system presumably worked fairly. Could someone paid by the firm alone objectively judge a worker's complaint? One arbitrator who worked for firms told me that he tried to be objective but that in the end he could never forget who was footing the bill. Even so, many labor experts favor ADR. As long as workers voluntarily agree to take their case to the company's arbitrator and the system meets quality standards for fairness, due process, and accountability to the goals and remedies in the relevant law, an ADR system offers many workers a better chance to resolve complaints about employer misconduct than going to court.

But then firms began to remove the voluntary choice part of the ADR system. Many insisted that, as a condition of employment, workers sign away their right to go to court in favor of the ADR system. This is reminiscent of the infamous "yellow dog" contracts of U.S. labor history, which firms used to force workers to agree not to join a union while employed by the firm. The United States outlawed the yellow dog contract in 1932. When courts began to consider the legality of yellow dog ADR, I was sure they would declare it illegal. I imagined that the courts would say that a firm could insist that workers use the ADR to deal with interpretation of company policy but could not insist that workers give up the right to go to court to protect rights at work that Congress had legislated. Some courts decided as I anticipated. Others did not. Then, in March 2001, the U.S. Supreme Court ruled 5–4 that employees cannot sue companies about their legal rights if the employees signed an arbitration agreement when they were hired.[14] More than 8 percent of American workers are now bound by arbitration agreements as a condition of their employment. Congress can pass protections, but in these firms the worker cannot go to court to enforce those protections. This effectively privatizes their legal rights at work.

The Trend: Squeeze the Suckers

In the heyday of welfare capitalism, firms regularly added fringe benefits to attract and retain workers. The Supreme Court ruled that pensions, health care, and other benefits are subject to collective bargaining, which made them part of normal compensation rather than gifts that firms bestow on workers. The tax system compelled firms to provide benefits to all workers since firms could deduct the costs of benefit packages as expenses before profits only if the package covered all workers.

Beginning in the 1980s and through the 2000s, the profit calculus of providing benefits changed; firms began to cut back on benefit programs, and they reduced one of the biggest items in compensation, defined-benefit pensions. Under this pension system, firms promised workers a monthly pension upon retirement and placed money in a pension fund to earn the returns to cover the promise. The money was workers' money since it was deferred compensation that otherwise would have shown up in the paycheck. Since pension moneys are not taxed until the worker receives the pension, both the worker and the firm enjoyed a tax break.

But pension funds ran into problems. There were financial abuses at some funds. And many firms did not put away enough money to pay the pensions they had promised. In 1974, following the collapse of the Studebaker automobile firm, whose underfunded pension plan left many older workers with little or no pensions, Congress enacted the Employment Retirement Income Securities Act (ERISA) to provide standards for pension funds.[15] It also established the Pension Benefit Guaranty Corporation, which insures pensions in case a firm goes bankrupt or otherwise cannot afford them. In 2006 Congress raised the charge for this insurance and enacted stricter rules for firms to fund their pension systems.

Because sizable proportions of the assets of pension funds are held in the stock market, these funds own about 24 percent of corporate equities, while individuals hold on the order of 21 percent in private retirement accounts, so that approximately 45 percent of domestic corporate equity is owned by workers as retirement savings.[16] Analysis of the way in which actuaries account for the risk of equities in pension funds indicates that they generally do not correctly account for the risks of equity in the funds' portfolios.[17] During the 1990s stock market boom, when pension funds were plush with assets, some firms decided that they did not have to contribute to the funds. Some promised larger pensions to workers. When the market fell, those pension funds suddenly went from being fully funded to meet their pension liabilities to underfunded. The firms had to take money from shareholders to make the pension funds whole. Many firms decided against bearing the risk of investing on behalf of workers and shifted their contributions to defined-contribution plans such as 401(k)s, where the firm and worker contribute money but the value of the pension depends on the value of those assets when the worker retires. Let the worker, not the firm, bear the risk.

Still, defined-benefit plans remain the primary form of pension for public-sector workers and for many union workers in the private sector. The largest pension fund in the United States, Calpers, is a defined-benefit fund. And even while firms shift regular employees to defined-contribution pension plans, many CEOs and top executives have defined-benefit pensions for themselves. Why bear the risk if you don't have to?

The rapidly rising costs of health benefits in the 1990s and 2000s created even greater problems than defined-benefit pensions for firms that bought health insurance for their workers. Health insurance is a defined benefit. The firm that offers health insurance has to pay the increases in the premiums over time. As the costs of insurance have risen—insurance for a family of four exceeded $10,000 per year by 2004—firms have had to squeeze other parts of their budget to meet the high insurance costs. One response to the higher price is to increase employee premiums—the contribution that workers make to take up the benefit. As the cost of premiums has risen, younger and lower-paid employees have been unable to afford health insurance, so that the proportion of workers with employment-based insurance fell from 69 percent in 1987 to 61 percent in 2004. In 2004 about four in five workers with family income twice the poverty level ($38,614 in 2004 for a family of four) had an employer plan compared to barely one-third of workers with lower family incomes.[18] Firms tried with limited success to control the costs of health care, using managed care systems and health maintenance organizations and offering workers different plans in the hope that their choices would discipline providers.

The net result is that fewer workers obtain health insurance from their workplace and workers pay a rising share of their health care bills directly. The national health system is in crisis. If I were an expert in health economics, I would add a chapter dealing entirely with this issue—it is that important for the job market—but I leave it to those with greater knowledge than mine.

Grab What You Can . . .

How much does the CEO of your firm make per year? One million dollars? Two million dollars? If you think those numbers are big, you are wrong. In the world of CEO compensation, a few million is small change. For years Michael Eisner of the Disney Corporation earned $100 million annually while company shares dropped in value.[19] In 1995 Disney hired Michael Ovitz as president of the firm and fired him fourteen months later with a $140 million severance pay. Ten million dollars a month in addition to regular pay and options for doing such a bad job that the firm fired him![20] Nice work if you can get it, and you can get it, or something close to it, if you get to the top of the corporate ladder.

119

These and other scandals in executive pay are meat to the radical fringe in America, but what does it mean when *Fortune* refers to the huge increase in top executive pay while company performance slumps as "The Great CEO Pay Heist"? Or when *Forbes*, invoking the French Bourbons, describes CEOs as taking what they can in the view that, après moi, le déluge? Or when the editor of the *Harvard Business Review* denounces the executives who ladled out stock options worth millions in the aftermath of the 9/11 attack on the United States, so that they could enrich themselves when the market recovered from the terrorism-induced fall in prices, as "sleaze balls and profiteering ghouls"?[21] *Fortune? Forbes? Harvard Business Review?* Something must be truly rotten in Denmark if these publications sound like *Mother Jones* or *Dollars and Cents*.

From the 1980s to the mid-2000s, the pay of top executives increased massively relative to that of average workers. In 1980 CEOs earned about 42 times as much as the average worker; thus, it took the average CEO a year to earn the lifetime earnings of the average worker. In 2005 CEOs earned from 262 to 431 times the pay of the average worker, depending on whose estimates of CEO pay we use.[22] It took about one or two months for the average CEO to make as much as the average worker earned in a lifetime. In 2005, while U.S. GDP per capita grew by 3 percent, the U.S. trade deficit increased, and workers worried about their jobs being offshored, the heads of America's five hundred largest companies received an aggregate 54 percent pay raise.[23] When management is in the driver's seat, management is amply rewarded.

CEOs in other countries also earn more than regular workers and have had more rapid increases in earnings than their employees, but the levels and differentials in pay are nothing like those in the United States. In many advanced countries, the ratio of CEO pay to the pay of ordinary workers even falls short of the 1980 ratio in the United States. One analysis comparing the pay of U.S. executives with that of U.K. executives found such huge differences that it referred to the former as princes and the latter as paupers.[24]

Besides compensation that includes huge expense accounts, access to corporate jets, and corporate apartments, much of the high earnings of CEOs and other top executives comes in stock options that pay off under a number of different scenarios: if the firm's share price rises; in so-called golden parachutes, so that if a CEO does poorly and is replaced by the firm, he or she still makes a fortune ($140 million in the case of Ovitz); and in lucrative defined-benefit retirement funds. Options allow their holders to buy shares at a given price, called the strike price; if the market price rises above that price, the holder can exercise the option (buy the shares) and then sell for a certain profit. Also, the holder is taxed at the lower capital gains rate rather than at the income tax rate paid by highly paid regular employees. In 1993 the Clinton administration encouraged stock options by capping the deductibility of salaries as corporate expenses at $1 million. Firms that paid executives over $1 million in salary had to pay that money out of after-tax profits, which cost them more than options that rewarded the executives the same amount.

The economically rational way to write options is to index the strike price to share prices in the stock market as a whole or to the share price of the industry in which the firm operates. This rewards management for doing better than the average. There is no point in paying large sums for improving share prices if share prices rise at the overall inflation rate of the stock market or if the firm's performance or share price falls short of that of its main competitors. But U.S. options are typically written in absolute value terms. Thus, if inflation raises all prices in the country, including shares, by 50 percent, or if a fall in the interest rate increases share prices, options increase in value even though the executive has done nothing. Nice work if you can get it, and you can get it if . . .

Options have given huge incentives to executives not only to act in the interests of shareholders, as intended, but also to find ways, legal or illegal, to profit from the options even when doing so goes against the interest of shareholders. The millions of dollars at stake create a powerful incentive for top managers to fudge financial reports, release good news around the times when they can cash in their options, and otherwise find ways to ensure that they cash in on the big bucks. When share prices fall and options go "under water," boards of directors, appointed by management, often reprice the options at lower prices. This means that if the value of the shares falls by 50 percent, so that management has little chance of cashing in the option, the board gives new options based on the new low price. If the share price then rises 20 percent from the low value, management cashes in even though shareholders have still lost value. Such a system reduces the incentive value of options.[25]

In the summer of 2006, a new scandal regarding options surfaced that shocked even aficionados of executive compensation. Some firms had gone beyond repricing options to backdating them. They would issue an option when stock prices were increasing and back-date the option as if it had been granted earlier when the prices were lower. The equivalent of counterfeiting money, this fraudulent practice destroys the legitimate purpose of options. At this writing, the Securities and Exchange Commission (SEC) and the Justice Department were investigating eighty or so companies for such fraudulent practices. Some firms have fired executives for backdating options. Others are defending themselves. One academic study estimates that upwards of one-third of large firms engaged in such fraud.[26]

Putting aside for the moment the fraud that underlies some top executive compensation, are CEOs worth 330 to 400 times the pay of regular workers? Some economists argue that they are indeed worth this level of compensation because they are ultimately responsible for how their firm performs. The larger the firm, the greater the potential contribution of executives, and executive pay varies strongly with size of firm. Some have even argued that CEOs are underpaid. If Super CEO comes to your firm and through his brilliant leadership doubles the value of the firm from $10 billion to $20 billion, that $10 billion increase is Super CEO's marginal product and that is what he should be paid. These economists stress that executives move from firm to firm, so that their pay reflects a market test. If a manager does well at firm A, then firm B will offer a higher compensation package to run it. Large "headhunting" firms search widely for the best managers for particular firms. An active competitive market ought to establish economically justifiable pay for top executives.

But other analysts note the close ties between boards of directors and top executives and wonder if the boards can make objective assessments of how much to pay CEOs and other top executives. The boards of directors rely on executive compensation consultants paid by the company to advise them on pay packages, just as they rely on accounting and auditing firms paid by the company to verify the books. The scandals of the 1990s and early 2000s proved that this system of corporate governance was rife with incompetence and criminality. In response, Congress enacted the Sarbanes-Oxley Act, the New York Stock Exchange added new listing requirements, and the Securities and Exchange Commission and other regulatory and monitoring groups added new rules and procedures to try to get boards and management to be more responsible and to ferret out criminal misconduct.[27] Given the abysmal record of boards appointed and dominated by CEOs in monitoring firm performance, why should anyone believe that the same boards were doing a great job in determining pay packages?

The problem in resolving this debate is that there is no simple objective measure of the productivity of CEOs and other executives—no batting averages or points scored per game, no papers published or records sold—to show how well a particular executive is doing. Maybe the firm is making money because the CEO made brilliant decisions and that $10 billion increase in value is due to the CEO. Or maybe the firm happened to be in the right spot at the right time, making purple hula hoops when those hoops suddenly became the rage. Maybe the firm is losing money but the CEO's brilliant decisions have staunched the losses. Anyone who wants to believe that CEOs and other executives are worth whatever they are paid can find economic analyses and interpretations of data that support this view.[28] But the malfeasance surrounding executive pay determination is not an interpretation. It is fact.

The model that I find most plausible for justifying extremely high pay for CEOs is the tournament model of pay and promotion.[29] According to this model, even if the CEO has modest or even negative value to the firm, the system of giving high rewards to the top executive makes the entire organization run better because it creates a tournament within the firm that leads lower-level management to go all out to get promoted to the exalted top spot. Forget the CEO—what he does is irrelevant. It's the incentive his excessive pay gives to the rest of the employees that justifies that pay.

But this model does not tell us whether paying the CEO twenty or forty or four hundred times the pay of the average worker induces the greatest effort by employees, which is the issue in contention. And economics says that tournaments that give many prizes induce more effort than those that concentrate on one big prize. Perhaps if some of the huge rewards at the top were offered as incentives to workers lower in the corporate hierarchy, firms would perform better. In fact, there is evidence that firms that share profits with workers are more productive than firms that differentiate sharply between management and employees.

. . . Or Share What You Can

Many U.S. companies relate employee earnings to the performance of the firm. The most popular way to do this is profit sharing, which either pays workers cash or puts the money or sometimes company stock into a retirement plan. Another way is gain sharing, which pays workers on the basis of their work unit's performance, over which they have more control than firm profits. Since 1974, U.S. tax law has given tax breaks to firms that establish employee stock ownership plans (ESOPs), which are funds that own shares of the firm in the name of workers. In addition, many large corporations make 401(k) plans a vehicle for employee ownership by matching employee contributions with company shares. High-tech firms pioneered the use of shares or stock options for their workers.

In 2002, 36 percent of employees were paid through a performance-sharing or employee ownership plan. Many of these were covered by two or more such plans. Six percent of all workers received part of their pay through a combination of profit sharing, employee ownership, and stock options. For most workers, the shared part of their compensation was a moderate part of their incomes—3 to 10 percent or so—but for some with employee ownership schemes, what they earned through ownership made up half or more of their income.[30]

Firms that share company success with workers do not do so for philanthropic reasons. They link the pay of workers to company performance for the same reason they give stock options to executives: to create incentives to improve the performance of the firm. The notion is that if workers have a piece of the action, they will be more motivated to work hard and to find ways to raise productivity or sales than if they are paid solely on an hourly or monthly basis. Firms that pay workers through "shared capitalist" compensation are more likely to devolve decisionmaking to workers so that employees will have both the incentive and the means to improve outcomes.

But will workers really try harder when their pay depends on the performance of their group or firm? Standard economic analysis suggests that they might instead choose to free-ride on the efforts of others. If you work with, say, ten workers and you gain just one-tenth of the extra income from your effort, why bother? If your neighbor tries hard, you get the same one-tenth with no effort. So let her do the work. If everyone thought like this, shared capitalist incentive systems would all run aground on a sea of free-riding behavior. But the facts are otherwise. Comparisons of the productivity of profit-sharing firms with the productivity of other firms find a moderate 2 to 3 percent advantage for the profit-sharers. Firms with employee ownership also tend to do better than others.[31] How do these firms overcome the free-rider problem and keep incentives high?

One way in which the shared capitalist systems overcome free-riding is through the greater willingness of workers in such systems to intervene with fellow employees who are not doing the job properly. In a set of surveys in the early 2000s, Joseph Blasi, Douglas Kruse, and I asked employees if they could tell whether a fellow worker was not working as hard or as well as he or she should and what they would do if they made such an observation. Most employees could tell who was working hard and who was goofing off. Some reported that they would speak to the shirker. Others said they would speak to the supervisor. Others said they would bring up the problem at meetings of their work group. And many said they had so acted in the past. Yet others said they would do nothing. What is critical for making shared capitalist arrangements work is that employees paid through profit or gain sharing or with an ownership stake were more likely to say they would take action against shirkers than were other workers. Workers who were involved in decisionmaking at the workplace as well as paid through some form of shared capitalism were especially likely to intervene with workers who were not doing their job.[32]

Do employees like shared capitalism? Receiving part of your pay in the form of profits or ownership makes your income more variable and risky. But you are also less likely to lose your job in an economic downturn. When demand falls for a firm's product and it has to reduce costs, some of that reduction occurs through lower profit shares to workers, which reduces the pressure on the firm to lay off workers. But the risks of ownership can be huge. When United Airlines went bankrupt, the pilots and machinists who had bought a majority share of the firm lost not only as capitalists but as workers. Still, a majority of workers say that they prefer to have some financial stake in their firm. And those in firms with shared capitalist arrangements are much less likely than others to say that they expect to leave their company in the next year.[33]

American Exceptionalism, Good and Bad

The most concise summary of what happens when management is in the driver's seat comes not from an economist or a business practitioner but from the poet Henry Wadsworth Longfellow, who wrote about his daughter Ella:

> There was a little girl,
> Who had a little curl,
> Right in the middle of her forehead,
> And when she was good,
> She was very, very good,
> But when she was bad she was horrid.

When U.S. managements are good, they are very good indeed to their employees. They manage in ways that create few problems, and they deal with the problems that arise efficaciously. They share

126

decisionmaking and the financial success of the firm with employees. But with no unions, limited government regulations, and ineffective corporate governance, when managements are bad, they are horrid. They treat workers poorly in the name of market realities. They find ways to pay themselves huge sums while squeezing the earnings of workers in the name of shareholder value. Worst of all, as the Enron, WorldCom, Tyco, Adelphia, and (name your favorite) scandals of the 2000s made clear, some CEOs and top managers use their power to defraud shareholders, workers, and customers.

Traditionally, labor specialists have not studied corporate governance and executive compensation. Unions bargained for wages and benefits and left issues regarding how management ran the firm or paid themselves to management. But the past twenty years have shown that when management is in the driver's seat, employees and those concerned with employee well-being have to make sure that firms are managed transparently and effectively. As an employee, you do not want to wake up one morning and find that the top executives of your firm have been studying from the Enron book of crooked management. It's your money they will be stealing, and your job they will be killing.

◈ CHAPTER 8 ◈

THE GREAT DOUBLING:
IS YOUR JOB GOING TO
BOMBAY OR BEIJING?

Before the collapse of communism in the Soviet Union, China's movement toward market capitalism, and India's decision to undertake market reforms and enter the global trading system, the global economy encompassed roughly half of the world's population—the advanced OECD countries, Latin America and the Caribbean, Africa, and some other parts of Asia. Workers in the United States, other higher-income countries, and market-oriented developing countries such as Mexico did not face competition from low-wage Chinese or Indian workers, nor from workers in the Soviet empire.

Then, in the 1990s, China, India, and the ex-Soviet bloc joined the global economy. Few analysts had expected the world to come together so quickly into a single economic world based on capitalism and markets. During the Cold War, it had seemed normal that the world was divided into competing economic systems with only loose connections to each other. When I was in Moscow in 1984 criticizing the problems of the U.S. labor market, I never thought that the Soviet system would implode a few years later, that China's Communist Party would introduce market capitalism and turn the country into the world's manufacturing center, or that India would give up its high tariffs and state-planned, highly regulated economy to join the global trading community.

Because these countries had approximately half of the world's population, their entry into the global economy effectively doubled the number of workers in the world's labor pool. Absent China, India, and the ex-Soviet bloc, there would have been about 1.46 billion workers in the global economy in 2000. The entry of those countries into the global economy raised the number of workers to 2.93 billion. Since twice 1.46 billion is 2.92 billion, I have called this "The Great Doubling."[1]

The doubling of the global workforce has presented the U.S. labor system with its greatest challenge since the Great Depression. If the U.S. labor market adjusts well to the change, the benefits of having virtually the whole human species on the same economic page will produce more rapid technological progress and improved living standards in the United States and in the rest of the world. If the United States does not adjust well, the next several decades will create economic problems for many workers in the United States and elsewhere and risk turning the country toward economic isolationism.

The Capital-to-Labor Balance

What impact might the doubling of the global workforce have on workers throughout the world? A simple thought experiment helps answer this question. Imagine what would happen if through some bizarre cloning experiment a mad economist (one of my colleagues, not me!) doubled the size of the U.S. workforce. Twice as many workers would seek employment from the same businesses. You don't need an economics PhD to see that this would be good for employers but terrible for workers. Wages would fall. Unemployment would rise. But now imagine that another mad economist knew some nanotechnology and found a bizarre way to increase the capital stock at the same time (more to my liking!). In this case, the doubling of the workforce would have a very different effect. In the simplest economic analysis, the effect of China, India, and the ex-Soviet bloc joining the global economy depends on how their entry altered the ratio of capital to labor in the global economy. This in turn depends on how much capital they brought with them when they entered the global system. Over the long run, the effect of the entry of these three countries into the global economy depends on their rates of savings and future capital formation.

When it first dawned on me that the "great doubling" was a significant event in economic history, I looked for estimates of the global capital stock that I could use to form a capital-to-labor ratio. There were none. There were estimates of capital stock for the United States and some other advanced countries, but no consistent dataset for the entire world. The researchers who produce the Penn World Tables, which has the best data on the aggregate economies of most countries in the world, told me that they were thinking about estimating capital stocks for countries but had not yet done so. Unwilling to wait for the definitive data (which at this writing are not available), I made my own estimates. I cumulated the Penn World table data on yearly investments to form capital stock measures country by country and then added the estimated stocks together into a measure of the global capital stock.[2] When the Penn World Tables team produces its own capital stock series, their estimates will dominate mine. But their estimates will undoubtedly give similar orders of magnitudes to mine and tell much the same story.

I estimated that the doubling of the global workforce reduced the ratio of capital to labor in the world economy in 2000 to 61 percent of what it would have been before China, India, and the ex-Soviet bloc joined the world economy.[3] The reason the global capital-to-labor ratio fell so much was that China, India, and the ex-Soviet bloc did not bring much capital with them. India had little capital because it was one of the poorest countries in the world. China was also very poor and destroyed some of its capital stock during the Maoist period. The Soviet empire was wealthier than China and India, but its capital was disproportionately invested in military goods and heavy industry instead of in computer-driven technologies or in the production and delivery of consumer products. Much of this capital stock was outmoded or so polluting as to be basically worthless.

The immediate impact of the entry of China, India, and the ex-Soviet bloc into the world economy was thus to reduce greatly the capital-to-labor ratio. This almost certainly shifted the global balance of power to capital. With a new supply of low-wage labor, firms could move facilities to lower-wage settings or threaten to do so if workers did not agree to wage concessions or changes in work conditions that were favorable to the firm. They could import products made by low-wage labor or subcontract parts of their production process to lower-cost locales. Employers in Central America, for example, told apparel workers that they had to work extra hours without any increase in weekly earnings to keep the business from moving to China. With wages in Central America three to four times those in China, the workers had little bargaining position.[4]

In the long run, China, India, and the ex-Soviet bloc will save and invest and contribute to the growth of the world capital stock. The World Bank estimates that China's savings rate is on the order of 40 to 50 percent, higher than the savings rate in most other countries; this will help increase global capital rapidly.[5] Though China is much poorer than the United States, it saves about as much as the United States in absolute terms. Still, it will take two to three decades to create a global capital-to-labor ratio equal to what it was before China, India, and the ex-Soviet bloc entered the world economy, and even longer to bring it to where it might have been absent their entry, assuming they maintain high savings rates. For the foreseeable future, then, labor markets outside of these countries will have to adjust to a relative shortfall of capital per worker and to the power this gives to firms in bargaining with workers.

Since capital will flow to China and India to employ their low-cost labor, the earnings of their workers should increase. In fact, the rate of economic growth in China and India zoomed once they adopted market economics and joined the global capitalist system, and wages and incomes rose substantially as well. The real earnings of urban manufacturing staff and workers in China increased by 6.7 percent per year between 1990 and 2002, more than doubling over that period. Poverty fell sharply in China despite its experience of one of the largest rises of inequality in the history of the world. Wages in India also appear to have risen rapidly—by about 4.3 percent a year, according to one World Bank study.[6]

But workers in many of the developing countries in Latin America, Africa, and Asia did not do well in the 1990s and early 2000s. Employment in many countries shifted from the formal sectors historically associated with economic advancement to informal sectors where work was precarious, wages and productivity were low, and occupational risks and hazards were great. The entry of China and India into the world economy turned many developing countries that had been the low-wage competitors of advanced countries into the high-wage competitors of China and India. Wages in Peru, El Salvador, Mexico, and South Africa, for example, are three to four times those in China and India.[7] These countries can no longer develop by producing generic low-wage goods and services for the global marketplace, which the "Washington consensus" model of development envisaged they would do.[8] The backlash against the orthodox World Bank/International Monetary Fund form of globalization in Latin America reflects this failure. Historically, no country has progressed economically by shifting its workers from formal-sector jobs to the informal sector.

The Effects of the Great Doubling on the United States

The typical American worker is far more skilled than the typical worker in a developing country. This difference in skills was in the forefront of the early 1990s U.S. debate over the impact of the NAFTA treaty. Proponents of the treaty argued that because the United States had a comparative advantage in producing high-tech goods, it would gain high-skilled jobs from increased trade with Mexico while exporting low-wage, less-skilled jobs. All U.S. workers had to do to benefit from this increased trade was to invest more in human capital.

The argument that the United States should gain skilled jobs while losing less-skilled jobs to Mexico would seem to apply even more strongly to trade with China and India. The average worker in China and India has lower skills than the average Mexican worker. From this perspective, Chinese and Indian workers are *complements to* rather than *substitutes for* American workers. Their joining the global labor pool should reduce the prices of the manufactured goods the United States buys and raise demand and prices for the high-tech goods and services the United States sells, which in turn should raise demand for educated labor in the United States. Lower prices for shoes and T-shirts and plastic toys and higher prices for semiconductors and business consulting and financial services would be in the interest of virtually all U.S. workers, save perhaps for the last shoemaker or seamstress.

The global labor market has not developed according to this scenario. Countries around the world, including India and China, have invested heavily in higher education, so that the number of college and university students and graduates outside the United States has grown rapidly relative to the number in the United States. In 1970 approximately 30 percent of university enrollments worldwide were in the United States. In 2000, 14 percent of university enrollments worldwide were in the United States. Similarly, the U.S. share of doctorates produced around the world has fallen from about 50 percent in the early 1970s to a projected share of 15 percent in 2010. Some of the growth of higher education overseas has been the result of European countries rebuilding their university systems following the destruction of World War II, and some is the result of Japan and Korea investing in university education. By the mid-2000s, several EU countries and Korea were sending a larger proportion of their young citizens to university than the United States was.[9] But much of the growth of higher education overseas is due to the growth of university education in developing countries, whose students made up nearly two-thirds of university enrollees in 2000. China has been in the forefront of this education boom: between 1999 and 2005, China increased the number of persons graduating with a bachelor's degree fivefold, to four million persons. By 2010, China will graduate more PhDs in science and engineering than the United States. The quality of university education is higher in the United States than in China, but quality will improve in China over time. India has produced many computer programmers and engineers.[10] And Indonesia, Brazil, Peru, Poland—name the country—more than doubled their university student enrollments in the 1980s and 1990s.[11]

Multinational firms have responded to the increased supply of highly educated workers by "global sourcing": looking for the best job candidates anywhere in the world and locating facilities, including high-tech R&D and production, where the supply of candidates is sufficient to get the work done at the lowest cost. Moving computer programming work or call centers to lower-wage countries is the natural economic response to the increased availability of educated labor in those countries. At the same time, the increased supply of educated persons outside the United States has combined with demands for highly skilled workers to produce a huge flow of immigrant scientists and engineers who have helped the United States maintain its position as the world leader in science and technology. In the dot-com and high-tech boom of the 1990s, the United States increased the employment of scientists and engineers greatly without increasing the number of graduates in science and engineering who were citizens or permanent residents and without raising the pay of scientists and engineers relative to that of other professions. Figure 8.1 shows the huge increase in the share of foreign-born workers in the science and engineering workforce from 1990 to 2000. Sixty percent of the growing number of PhD scientists and engineers were foreign-born, with the largest numbers coming from China and India. Some of the foreign-born obtained their education in the United States and stayed to work. But most of those with a BS degree, and roughly half of those with a higher degree, graduated overseas and came to fill jobs. As long as the United States is an attractive place to work and is open to immigration, the increased supply of science and engineering graduates overseas implies that this country *cannot* experience a shortage in the science and engineering workforce.

From the perspective of highly educated U.S. workers, however, both the global sourcing of skilled jobs to low-wage countries and the immigration of highly educated workers to the United States reduce their economic prospects. It gainsays the notion that skilled Americans need not worry about competition from skilled workers in lower-income countries. If you study or work in science and engineering, where knowledge is universal, you should worry. Your job may not go to Bombay or Beijing, but you will be competing with persons from those countries and other low-wage countries in the market.

Figure 8.1   The Change in the Number of Foreign-Born Science
and Engineering Workers During the 1990s
Economic Boom

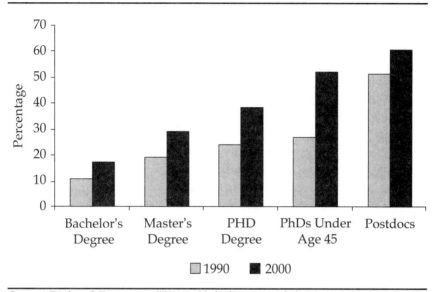

Source: Richard Freeman, "Does Globalization of the Scientific/Engineering Workforce Threaten U.S. Economic Leadership?" *Innovation Policy and the Economy* 6(2006): 123–58.

The Challenge of Human Resource Leapfrogging

Comparative advantage, comparative advantage, wherefore art thou, O comparative advantage?

Economists use the "North-South" product cycle model to analyze trading patterns between advanced and developing countries when technology is a critical element in trade.[12] This model assumes that the advanced countries (the "North") have highly skilled workers who enable it to monopolize cutting-edge innovative sectors while the developing countries (the "South") produce traditional lower-tech products. Workers in the North benefit from their country's monopoly on high-tech. The greater the rate of technological advance and the slower the spread of the newest technology to low-wage countries, the higher paid are workers in the North relative to workers in the South.

In such a model, the spread of higher education and modern technology to low-wage countries can reduce advanced countries' comparative advantage in high-tech and adversely affect workers in the advanced countries. In 2004, as many engineers and computer specialists worried that their employer might offshore their job to a developing country, Paul Samuelson reminded economists that a country with a comparative advantage in a given sector can suffer economic loss when another country competes successfully in that sector.[13] The new competitor increases supplies, which should reduce the price of the sector and the income for the original exporter. If the new competitor gains a large market share, many workers have to shift to less desirable sectors—those with a lower chance for productivity growth, fewer good jobs, and so on. Some trade specialists reacted negatively to Samuelson's comment. What he said was well known to them but irrelevant. In the real world it would never happen.[14]

Samuelson was right, and his critics were wrong. The assumption underlying the North-South model, that only advanced countries have the educated workforce necessary for competing with the United States, is no longer true. Low-income China has moved rapidly up the technological ladder, increased its high-tech exports, and achieved a significant position in research in what many believe will be the next big industrial technology—nanotechnology. Over 750 multinational firms have set up R&D facilities in China. China's share of scientific research papers has risen greatly.[15] India has not invested as much in science and engineering as China, but it has achieved a strong international position in information technology, also attracting major R&D investments, particularly in Bangalore.

How can lower-income countries with many less-educated peasants and relatively few scientists and engineers compete in high-tech?

By graduating large absolute numbers of scientists and engineers. It is not the number of engineers per capita that produces a technological breakthrough, but the total number of engineers working on the problem. China and India are gaining large footprints in high-tech because, with their billion-plus populations, they can produce as many or more highly educated scientists and engineers as advanced countries even though the bulk of their workforce is less skilled. I have called the process of moving up the technological ladder by educating large numbers of students in science and engineering "human resource leapfrogging," since it uses human resources to leapfrog comparative advantage from low-tech to high-tech sectors. The combination of low wages and highly educated workers in these large populous countries makes them formidable competitors for an advanced country.

At the same time, the development of computers and the Internet enhances the potential for firms to move work to low-cost operations. Business experts report that if work is digital—as is at least 10 percent of employment in the United States—it can and eventually will be offshored to low-wage, highly educated workers in developing countries. The most powerful statement by a business group on this issue was made in 2005 by the Institute of Directors in the United Kingdom:

> The availability of high-speed, low-cost communications, coupled with the rise in high-level skills in developing countries meant off shoring has become an attractive option outside the manufacturing industry. Britain has seen call centres and IT support move away from Britain, but now creative services such as design and advertising work are being outsourced. There is more to come. In theory, anything that does not demand physical contact with a customer can be outsourced to anywhere on the globe. For many U.K. businesses this presents new opportunities, for others it represents a serious threat. But welcome it or fear it, it is happening anyway, and we had better get used to it.[16]

Replace "Britain" and "U.K." with "the United States," and "business" with "worker," and this statement applies as much or more to the situation facing U.S. workers. The bottom line is that the spread of modern technology and education to China and India will undo some of the American advantage in high-tech innovation and production and place competitive pressures on U.S. workers. Eventually, the wages of workers in China and India will approach those in the United States, as have the wages of European, Japanese, and to some extent Korean workers, but that is a long way off. Until then, the challenge for American workers is to obtain work skills that differ sufficiently from those being produced in huge numbers overseas to keep U.S. wages high. The challenge to U.S. policymakers and firms is to invest in science and technology so that the country maintains comparative advantage in enough high-tech areas to keep it in the forefront of the world economy in the face of low-wage competitors.

The Transition to a Truly Global Labor Market

Absorbing the huge workforces of China, India, and potentially other successful developing countries into global capitalism will take the global economy a long time. It took thirty or so years for Western Europe and Japan to reach technological, economic, and wage parity with the United States. It took Korea about fifty years to move from being one of the poorest economies in the world to the second rung of advanced economies. If China keeps its economy growing rapidly and wages double every decade, as they did in the 1990s, Chinese wages will approach the levels that the United States has today in about thirty years. Indian wages will take longer to reach U.S. levels. The transition to a global labor market with roughly comparable living standards for workers will take at least half a century and probably longer. This is a long transition, and that means that there will be plenty of opportunity for things to go wrong in various ways for U.S. workers and for others as well.

How the United States fares in the transition will depend on a race between labor market factors that improve living standards and factors that reduce those standards. On the improvement side is the likelihood that more highly educated workers making advances in science and technology will raise productivity rates and that the price of goods will be lower because they will be made by lower-wage workers overseas. On the reduction side are the labor market pressures from those overseas workers to reduce pay in the United States, as well as the possible worsening U.S. terms of trade and loss of comparative advantage in the high-tech industries that offer the greatest prospects for productivity advances and the most desirable jobs.

Which set of forces wins the race depends in part on the economic and labor market policies that countries, the international community, unions, and firms choose to guide the transition. I can envisage both a good transition scenario and a bad transition scenario.

In the good transition, India, China, and other low-wage countries close the gap with the United States and other advanced countries in the wages paid their workers as well as in their technological competence. Their scientists, engineers, and entrepreneurs develop and produce new and better products for the global economy, thus enabling them to reduce the costs of production and to dominate the declining terms of trade in the advanced countries so that their living standards improve. The United States (and other advanced countries) retains comparative advantage in enough leading sectors or niches of sectors to remain a global hub in the development of technology. The world savings rate rises so that the global capital-to-labor ratio increases rapidly. As U.S. GDP grows, the country distributes some of the growth in national output through increased social services and social infrastructure—national health insurance, for instance—or through earned income tax credits so that living standards rise even for workers whose wages are constrained by low-wage competitors.

In the bad transition, China and India develop enclave economies in which only their highest-earning modern-sector workers benefit from economic growth while the rural poor remain low-paid and a sufficient threat to less-skilled urban workers that wages grow slowly. This places great pressure on labor markets in the United States and other advanced countries. The global capital stock grows slowly as Americans maintain high consumption by keeping savings low. At some point U.S. citizens begin to blame globalization for economic problems and try to abort the transition and introduce trade barriers and limit the transfer of technology. To add to the nightmare, huge within-country inequalities in China, India, and other countries produce social disorder that creates chaos or gets suppressed by a global "super-elite" who use their wealth and power to control a mass of struggling poor. The bad transition scenario resembles some recalcitrant Marxist's vision of global capitalism.

Conclusion

The triumph of global capitalism has spread modern technology and business practices to most of humanity and brought workers around the world closer to competing in the same labor market, either through immigration or through the flows of capital and trade. The overriding goal of labor market policy around the world as the global economy absorbs the huge workforces of China, India, and the ex-Soviet bloc should be to make this process go as smoothly as possible. This will require increased sharing of the benefits and costs of this major economic transformation in the United States, along lines I lay out in the concluding chapter. The competitive market will need some help in making a smooth transition to a new global labor market.

❧ CHAPTER 9 ❧

HELPING THE INVISIBLE HAND DO BETTER

Nothing irritated John Dunlop, former secretary of Labor, dean of faculty at Harvard, and my mentor as labor economist at Harvard, as much as academics tacking obiter dicta policy suggestions on to the end of their specialized analyses without giving them the critical attention that they had given to the rest of their study. When I was a student, Dunlop would rail about research that focused on one aspect of a problem but ignored other aspects, that failed to consider the political realities in changing policies, and that ignored the problems of implementation. He viewed ideas by academics that bore no line responsibility for policies as "blue sky" dreaming.

Mea culpa. As I noted at the outset of *America Works*, this chapter differs from the rest of the book. It is normative and prescriptive rather than analytic. It takes as given the impressive rates of employment, productivity growth, and economic responsiveness that the U.S. labor market delivered in the 1990s and 2000s, and it also takes as given the huge inequality and the failure to deliver the benefits of rapid growth to most workers and to give workers the voice they want at their workplaces. Given these disparate outcomes, the question becomes: Can the United States do better? Are there labor market reforms and policies that can mitigate the failures of the exceptional labor market while maintaining its successes?

The growing influence of globalization on economic outcomes documented in chapter 8 makes it more important and more difficult to find such policies. The doubling of the global workforce gives greater power to capital and management than in the past.

Given the way management operates when it is in the driver's seat, such power risks exacerbating inequality in the United States between the owners of capital and top management and the rest of the workforce, if not between highly educated and less-educated workers, both of whom face increased competition from workers overseas. Some of my conservative colleagues believe that Americans have no choice but to "suck it up" and accept growing inequality and insecurity at work, though they would never use such strong language. For them, the invisible hand has spoken, and that is what it says. You better do what capital wants, or you will be in an even worse state. Others believe that the cure for the weaknesses of America's exceptional labor market is to go further down the road toward laissez-faire. Eliminate what is left of the unions, reduce government protections further, let all workers deal with their problems on their own, and somehow or other the average worker's position will improve.

I reject these prescriptions for doing nothing. Doing nothing but hoping that the unfettered market will suddenly turn in favor of workers will not produce the more even distribution of economic outcomes that most Americans, from conservatives to progressives, would like to see. For three or so decades, with some modest exceptions, the country has tried trickle-down economics, and only in the peak of the late 1990s boom did anything much reach regular workers. The market that best fits the invisible hand model, the financial market, requires considerable government oversight and institutional rules to provide the transparency and trust necessary to produce efficient outcomes. Shareholders have to organize and battle to protect their interests against many of the managements that purportedly represent them. If financial markets need institutional oversight and transparency to work for the benefit of all, so too do labor markets and the institutions that govern labor and management relations. So what might mitigate the weaknesses of the exceptional labor market while preserving its strengths?

I sketch out nine possible reforms that seek to strengthen the position of U.S. workers by supplementing market forces with institutions and policies that will better enable them to navigate the labor market in an era of massive globalization. My general assumption in making these suggestions is that policies whose primary effect is to help ordinary citizens are more likely to benefit those citizens than trickle-down policies whose primary effect is to enrich the super-wealthy.

The chapter is brief, because it would require another book to meet the Dunlop critique and give a full analysis of these policies. With modern tools of analysis, I would want to develop artificial agent simulations of the possible effects of the policies under alternative economic scenarios (at which Dunlop would look askance),[1] come up with econometric estimates of the magnitude of key parameters (which he would find useful), and hold extensive discussions with labor, management, and government decisionmakers (to which he would give the most credence). Even though my suggestions are brief and do not meet the Dunlop tests of stringent feasibility, I believe that there is virtue in placing them in the arena of public discourse. If you do not like the weaknesses that the U.S. labor market has developed but find my proposals too feeble or too radical, offer your own. To paraphrase the great wandering mathematician Paul Erdös, our minds should be open—in this case not to new mathematics but to diverse plans to improve the operation of the labor market and the well-being of all American workers.[2]

My proposals consist of a two-part strategy. Part one is to provide workers and firms with tools that will help them navigate the labor market and produce better market outcomes. Many will find at least some of these policies attractive, but they cost money, which requires taxes, and taxes incur "deadweight losses" that effectively add to the cost of the programs.[3] In addition, most of the extra taxes would presumably come from the wealthy, while most of the benefits would go to ordinary citizens. Thus, these are not "win-win" strategies: wealthy Americans may end up less well off. Part two calls for changes in some of the rules governing labor market institutions to favor workers and to encourage unions and other worker-friendly groups to risk more activist and innovative policies to redistribute decisionmaking and rights at work toward ordinary workers. These changes would also incur costs. Some of my conservative friends will object to these proposals for fear that they would weaken responsiveness to market forces. But the evidence reviewed in this book is that American workers are highly responsive to market realities. The market does not speak solely to the wealthy and powerful.

Five Ways to Help Workers and Firms

The U.S. labor market is closer to the ideal model than labor markets in virtually any other advanced country, but it still does not operate in perfect accord with the invisible hand model. This book has stressed the huge dispersion of pay among observationally equivalent workers, the increases of productivity that fail to show up in the earnings of the vast bulk of the population, and management's penchant for enriching management. In part, these problems reflect weaknesses in the perfect market model that modern economic analysis seeks to remedy: individual concerns over "fairness" in decisionmaking and distribution; imperfect information and responses to information; and individual abuse of authority within organizations. Here are five ways to enable workers and firms to operate more effectively in the labor market.

1. A large increase in spending on R&D and fellowship support of students in science and engineering. The United States has attained a unique position in the global economy as the leading scientific and technological center. This gives the country a comparative advantage in high-technology industries and other sectors, such as university education, that allows it to compete with low-wage countries in global markets. Underlying the U.S. position is a highly developed university system, funded in large part by governments, and investment in basic research and development, funded in large part by the federal government. Increases in government spending—for fellowships for graduate study and for R&D—could increase the demand and supply for highly educated labor while helping maintain U.S. leadership in technology and science.[4] In 2006 both political parties endorsed these types of proposals. With just a month or so of the billions spent on the war in Iraq allocated to improving the country's R&D and its science and engineering workforce, the United States could raise the economic prospects of all citizens. By devoting federal research moneys to energy and environmental issues rather than a manned space trip to Mars or the moon, the government could better position the U.S. economy to continue its rapid growth and develop an appropriate niche for U.S. workers to compete globally.

2. *Supplements to the pay of low-wage workers or families that would "make work pay more," even for those with limited skills.* In even the best-functioning labor market, some workers have low productivity and low earnings that require institutional intervention to reach some socially acceptable minimum. The trick is to make the social safety net a safety net for work rather than an incentive to stay on a dole—workfare not welfare. As described earlier in the book, the United States has two reasonably successful programs that do this: the Earned Income Tax Credit (including a variant currently labeled "wage insurance") and the minimum wage.[5] Neither is perfect. Both must be paid for, however, either by taxes (the EITC) or by higher prices for goods and services or lower profits (the minimum wage). The critical issue is to find the levels to which they can be raised without incurring greater costs on the economy than benefits.

3. *Provision of a wider basket of public goods and services to all citizens, irrespective of their labor market position.* The country provides police protection, highways, public schools, parks, libraries, and defense for all citizens as public goods. The natural extension is to provide health insurance through a national scheme that would take the cost of providing medical insurance off the books of firms. Done right, this could reduce the burden of the extraordinarily expensive U.S. health care system and lower the marginal cost of hiring labor. Here we know from past efforts to reform health care that the details are critical. President Clinton was elected with a mandate to develop a health insurance system covering all Americans, but his proposal was so poorly structured that virtually every expert with knowledge of the health care system, including many of the administration's advisers, hoped that Congress would reject it, which it did. But this failure did not solve the problem. As noted earlier in the book, the problem remains.

4. *Public investments in national infrastructure and the environment.* U.S. workers cannot compete in the global market on the basis of wages. They have to have higher productivity than workers over-

145

seas. Some of this comes from human capital and some from the investments of firms, but some also comes from public investments in effective mass transit systems and from investments in and regulations for environmentally friendly production that enhances the attractiveness of our cities to multinational firms and globally mobile workers. Again, these are market-enhancing investments, and the details are critical. The bridge to nowhere in Alaska is not a market-enhancing investment in public infrastructure.[6]

5. *Increased profit sharing and employee stock ownership.* Persons with capital assets, physical and human, have done best in the U.S. economy. Chapter 7 pointed out that, according to most studies, firms that share some of their profits with workers perform modestly better (and certainly not worse) than those that do not share rewards with workers. Employee stock ownership plans, which are tax-advantaged, have millions of employee participants, but policy initiatives to expand employee sharing in the gains of their firms and in the risks are few and far between. Since tax breaks risk encouraging firms to undertake more "shared capitalism" simply to get the break rather than to improve their operations, I favor establishing a federal agency designed to gather information, publicize best practices, and otherwise aid firms that choose to pay workers in these ways, much as the Small Business Administration assists small firms in the marketplace.

Four Ways to Improve the "Property Rights" of Workers

Economic analysis says that markets can operate efficiently under almost any reasonable set of property rights and decisionmaking authority.[7] To the extent that this is true, changes in property rights favorable to workers could improve their economic well-being without having an impact on economic efficiency. Here are four ways to shift the ownership of property and the control of decisionmaking to workers.

6. *Greater worker control of worker assets.* Employees own but do not control a large share of equity through their retirement plans. Since activist pension funds have taken a lead in efforts to reform

corporate governance, such policies are likely to benefit shareholders broadly. Pension funds that are more responsive to workers could be expected to make greater investment in metropolitan cores—where many workers with pension assets reside.

7. *Expanded choice of modes of representation for workers beyond the dichotomy between a collective bargaining contract and nothing.* The requirement that unions win the support of a majority of workers at particular workplaces and the outlawing of other forms of employee workplace activity or organization for fear that they will become company unions are the mainstays of a system that, as noted in chapter 5, has failed American workers and firms. Since there is uncertainty about the impacts of labor law reform, I favor increasing the authority to experiment with alternative regulations.[8] Without any changes in labor laws, however, workers and unions can pursue the innovative open-source union form described in that chapter. The free-market solution to an imbalance between capital and labor is to enhance the ability of labor to take care of itself, as part owners of capital and as an organized entity, union or nonunion, inside firms.

8. *Tax breaks for offering stock options to all workers proportionate with their income.* As part of a policy to increase workers' stakes in their firm and to limit executive abuse of stock options, I would apply the same basic rule to stock options that the federal government applies to health and pension benefits: the benefit has to be available to all workers proportionate to their income for it to receive favorable tax treatment as a deduction in costs from profits.

9. *Certification or licensing of persons who serve on corporate boards.* The boards of directors of U.S. firms play an important role in monitoring management's performance and determining compensation. But there are no criteria for serving on boards, and corporations do not search openly for the most qualified candidates, as they do for other jobs. Everything is done through old boy networks; as a result, persons who cannot read corporate balance sheets or understand the technologies of the firm can sit on boards. To improve the quality of board members, I would have a certification procedure that would assure shareholders and workers that board members have the relevant skills to assess managerial per-

formance. Management could appoint board members who lacked the certificate, but this would signal to shareholders that they were selecting persons without the appropriate knowledge and training. The United States licenses hundreds of occupations that have much less impact on the economy, so this is a relatively modest proposal—but one that could improve both corporate governance and the well-being of workers within a firm.

The unifying goal of these strategies to help the U.S. labor market distribute the benefits of economic progress to all persons is not only to enable ordinary workers to improve their well-being but to lean against the power of those who control great assets while being respectful of the successes of the labor market in employment and productivity. Increasing the returns to work for the lower-paid, expanding the employment property rights and capital ownership of all workers, and raising productivity through public as well as private investments should be the goals of all persons who seek to encourage the U.S. labor market to reach its full potential.

I haven't been back to Moscow for many years; the Russian brand of capitalism, with high inequality, power controlled from the center, and a decaying university and research system, does not appeal to me. But when I return there someday, and whenever I go anywhere overseas, I would love to be able to say that I once had critical views of the U.S. labor market, but no longer; now I want only to sing its praises. For all my dismal science training, I am convinced that the United States can find the policies to gainsay my criticisms and put me out of the critic business. Huzzah for the future reforms of our labor market and for a less unequal distribution of income and power.

Notes

Introduction

1. Maxwell Smart was the star spy in a 1960s satire of secret agent movies and television shows. The villainous organization against which Smart worked was KAOS. The show was filled with wisecracks and catchphrases. See Wikipedia, "Get Smart," http://en .wikipedia.org/wiki/Get_Smart.
2. See Wikipedia, "American Exceptionalism," http://en.wikipedia .org/wiki/American_exceptionalism; see also Lipset, *American Exceptionalism*.
3. Freeman, *Working Under Different Rules*; see also the NBER Comparative Labor Series, published by the University of Chicago Press, which compares the labor markets and social protections of advanced countries.
4. *Dragnet* was probably the most famous and influential police drama series on radio or television. It ran in the 1950s and 1960s and produced the catchphrase "just the facts, ma'am"; see Wikipedia, "Dragnet," http://en.wikipedia.org/wiki/Dragnet_%28series%29.
5. For a description of the list, including a list of the top nine wealthiest in 2006, see Wikipedia, "Forbes 400," http://en.wikipedia.org/ wiki/Forbes_400; see also Lombardi, "How to Marry a Billionaire?"

Chapter 1

1. Gwartney and Lawson, "Economic Freedom of the World: 2006 Annual Report," 5.
2. Elsewhere (Freeman, "Varieties of Labor Market Institutions and Economic Performance"), I have examined the statistical relations between components of the index of economic freedom and the level of GDP per capita and economic growth. The labor index does not have the same positive relation to GDP or the growth of GDP as the overall index does, but it is highly negatively correlated with levels of inequality. This suggests that the index is a better measure of the tilt in a country's institutions toward the distribution of income than of its economic efficiency.
3. Figure 1.1 covers the major advanced countries. It leaves out two

149

places that have higher labor regulation scores than the United States: Iceland (8.0 versus 7.9 for the United States) and Hong Kong (8.6). It also leaves out Singapore and Taiwan, both of which have lower scores than the United States.

4. For more information, see the Labor and Worklife Program website, http://www.law.harvard.edu/programs/lwp/LWPclmp.html#gls.

5. Chor and Freeman, "The 2004 Global Labor Survey."

6. The OECD publishes data on union density and collective bargaining coverage intermittently in its *Employment Outlook*; see *Employment Outlook 2004*, ch. 3, for the latest data.

7. Other OECD data show the United States having the second-lowest share of expenditures, with Ireland having the lowest.

8. For an analysis of the labor institutions in the English-speaking countries, see Freeman, Boxall, and Haynes, *What Workers Say*.

9. As reported in European Commission, "European Year of Workers' Mobility 2006."

10. See Osawa and Kingston, "Flexibility and Inspiration."

11. The European data are from the 2003 EU labor force survey available from European Commission, "European Year of Workers' Mobility 2006." The U.S. data are from Moscarini and Thomsson, "Occupational and Job Mobility in the United States."

12. The comparisons of the percentages changing residence are from "Labor Markets in the Twenty-first Century," a joint American and EU conference (Washington: U.S. Department of Labor, Bureau of International Labor Affairs, September 2002). Gross and net flows for the population age fifteen to sixty-four are estimated from OECD, *Employment Outlook 2005*, ch. 2, chart 2.7; figures for the EU are taken as the average of eight advanced Western European countries.

13. OECD, *Employment Outlook 2004*, chart 2.4.

14. Calculated from OECD, *Employment Outlook 2005*, table G (for incidence of long-term unemployment) and table A (for rate of unemployment).

15. OECD, *Employment Outlook 2006*, table 3.2.

16. See Columbia University, "U.S. Unemployment Insurance."

17. OECD, *Employment Outlook 2004*, chart 2.4. For the pattern of flows into and out of unemployment in 1992, see Martin, "The Extent of High Unemployment in OECD Countries," chart 4.

18. OECD, *Employment Outlook 1994*, ch. 3; OECD, *Employment Outlook 1987*, ch. 4.

19. Chi, Freeman, and Kleiner, "Does Voluntary Job Changing Improve Work Satisfaction?"

20. Viscusi, *Employment Hazards.*
21. Botero, Djankov, Porta, and Lopez-De-Silanes, "The Regulation of Labor."
22. See Wikipedia, "American Exceptionalism," http://en.wikipedia .org/wiki/Americentric.
23. See Keely, "American Exceptionalism."
24. Freeman, "War of the Models."

Chapter 2

1. The 1970 hours are taken from OECD, *Employment Outlook 1993*, table B (total employment with dependent employment figures used for Germany). The 2005 hours are taken from OECD, *Employment Outlook 2006*, table F. The European countries are Finland, Sweden, Norway, France, Germany, and Italy. The European averages are weighted averages based on employment reported in OECD, *Employment Outlook 1992* for 1989.
2. Council of Economic Advisers, *Economic Report of the President 2006*, table B-42. Unemployment rates for the 1950s are taken from *Economic Report of the President 1966*, table C-22, available at: http://fraser .stlouisfed.org/publications/ERP/page/18/1199/download/18.pdf.
3. Tabulated from Council of Economic Advisers, *Economic Report of the President 2006*, table B-36. In 1992 there were 118.5 million U.S. civilians employed; in 2000 136.9 million civilians were employed.
4. Tabulated from ibid., table B-39.
5. In Freeman and Schettkat, "Marketization of Household Production," table 3, Ronald Schettkat and I contrast hours of work in the market and hours of work in household production.
6. Much of the evidence here is taken from ibid.
7. Freeman and Schettkat ("Marketization of Household Production") show that European women actually spend more hours working in total than American women, but the differences are small.
8. See U.S. Department of Labor, "Work at Home in 2004," table 6.
9. For a detailed analysis of the marketization hypothesis, see Freeman and Schettkat, "Marketization of Household Production."
10. In 2003, 775,000 women earned a bachelor's degree in the United States, compared to 573,000 men; see U.S. Bureau of the Census, table 286, http://www.census.gov/compendia/statab/tables/06s0286.xls.
11. Researchers have examined the effects of day care as opposed to parental care on children. Some studies find modest negative effects, but the overall results suggest that day care does not have a great im-

pact on children, though the quality of day care does. See Phillips and Bridgman, National Academy of Sciences, *New Findings on Children, Families, and Economic Self-sufficiency*. For a summary of some of this work, see Lalli, "The Effects of Day Care on Children's Emotional, Cognitive, and Social Development."

12. Camarota, "A Jobless Recovery?," table 1.
13. See Freeman, "People Flows in Globalization."
14. Finn, "Stay Rates of Foreign Doctorate Recipients from U.S. Universities, 2003."
15. Freeman, "Does Globalization of the Scientific/Engineering Workforce Threaten U.S. Economic Leadership?"
16. Tabulated from Ruggles et al., *Integrated Public Use Microdata Series: Version 3.0*.
17. For a period, Hardy would have not been able to break into the lineup of any Washington team. In 1972 the Senators of Joe Hardy's day moved to Texas, where they became the Texas Rangers. Washington did not have a team until 2005 when the Montreal Expos moved to Washington and became the Nationals.
18. Passell, "The Size and Characteristics of the Unauthorized Migrant Population in the U.S."
19. U.S. National Commission on Technology, Automation, and Economic Progress, *Technology and the American Economy*.
20. If there is only one type of labor, labor must benefit from the increase in productivity; see Simon, *The Shape of Automation for Men and Management*, ch. 1.
21. Wikipedia, "Solow Computer Paradox," http://en.wikipedia.org/wiki/Solow_computer_paradox.
22. Estimated from U.S. Department of Labor, Bureau of Labor Statistics, production worker and employee tables, available at: http://www.bls.gov/ces/home.htm#tables.
23. All data from Council of Economic Advisers, *Economic Report of the President 2006*. Real average hourly earnings are from table B-47; productivity estimated by dividing real GDP by civilian employment in 1973 and 2005. GDP figures are from table B-2, and employment figures are from table B-36.
24. The median earnings are for full-time workers. The earnings figures are from U.S. Bureau of the Census, *U.S. Statistical Abstract*, 1976, table 608, and 2006, table 638. The CPI are from Council of Economic Advisers, *Economic Report of the President 2006*, table B-60.
25. The most accessible data relate to manufacturing. OECD statistics

show that from 1970 to 2000 real earnings in manufacturing increased in nine of ten countries for which it had data and that from 1989 to 2000 real earnings in manufacturing increased in fourteen of sixteen countries for which it had data. The United States was one exception in both periods, while Australia also had a decline in real earnings in the shorter period. From 1970 to 2000, average earnings rose by 2.1 percent per year in France, by 1.8 percent in Germany, and by 2.0 percent in Japan. OECD, *Historical Statistics 1970–2000*, table 8.2.

26. These data are from U.S. Department of Commerce, *National Income and Product Accounts*, table 1.12.
27. Greenhouse and Leonhard, "Real Wages Fail to Match a Rise in Productivity."
28. For instance, Lawrence Lindsey pointed out that persons earning $100,000 or more, who make up the upper 10 percent of the income distribution, paid 61.9 percent of taxes. Earlier, Lindsey had noted that the upper 1 percent of families were paying an increasing proportion of taxes, taking the burden off the rest of society. See Nasar, "Who Paid the Most Taxes in the 1980s."
29. The argument that because the rich pay a large share of taxes, they will inevitably get a large share of any tax cut is not correct. The country could give tax cuts as lump sum payments to taxpayers, the way Alaska distributes the earnings from its oil fund to every person in the state regardless of their income; it could also either raise the level below which workers pay no taxes or increase the negative income tax associated with the Earned Income Tax Credit.
30. U.S. Bureau of the Census, *2005 Annual Social and Economic (ASEC) Supplement*, appendix F.
31. Tabulated from Dew-Becker and Gordon, "Where Did the Productivity Growth Go?," tables 8 and 9.
32. Jones, "Forbes 400 Richest Americans Are All Billionaires This Year."
33. The CPI is calculated on the basis of the prices paid by urban consumers for a fixed basis of goods that they consume. The GDP deflator is calculated on the basis of prices for domestically produced goods and services, including investment goods and other goods and services that consumers do not purchase, relative to the previous period. The two series differ for a variety of reasons, such as changes in the price of imports, which affect the CPI directly but do not affect the GDP deflator directly.

Chapter 3

1. Freeman, *The Overeducated American*. The cobweb model in the appendix to the book predicted that the low return to college in the early 1970s would rise, but I was sufficiently uncertain about forecasting such a change that I played down this part of the analysis. My analysis focused on the earnings of college graduates, and I simply assumed that the real earnings of nongraduates would rise at their historic rate. What I failed to see then was the divergence between the growth of productivity and the growth of real wages.

2. Tabulated from Dew-Becker and Gordon, "Where Did the Productivity Growth Go?," table 9. The share of the lower 80 percent in 1972 was 54.9 percent, while the share of the upper 1 percent was 15.4 percent.

3. Tabulated from Economic Policy Institute, "Datazone." I have taken "Ronald Reagan inequality" to be the distribution of income in 1984, when families in the lower 80 percent had 57 percent of family income. If that distribution had held in 2004, families in the lower 20 percent would have earned 20 percent higher income, those in the next 20 percent would have had 15 percent higher income, those in the next 20 percent would have had 10 percent higher income, and those in the next 20 percent would have had 6 percent higher income. Applying the 1984 distribution to 2004 family incomes raises the average income for the bottom 80 percent from $44,874 to $49,184.

4. Tabulated from Dew-Becker and Gordon, "Where Did the Productivity Growth Go?," table 9. I take the share of the lower 80 percent in 2001 as 43.6 percent while the share of the upper 1 percent was 35.6 percent.

5. Freeman, "How Labor Fares in Advanced Countries."

6. Ibid., 13.

7. CIA, "Field Listing: Distribution of Family Income: Gini Coefficient." I have examined estimated Gini coefficients from other sources and find similar patterns.

8. Devroye and Freeman, "Does Inequality of Skills Explain Inequality of Earnings Across Advanced Countries?"

9. This is true when inequality is measured in relative terms. Whether the CEO makes ten times or one hundred times the pay of the average worker, as long as the ratio of their earnings remains the same, then a 20 percent increase in CEO pay will be matched by a 20 percent increase in the average worker's pay. The absolute difference in their pay will widen more when the CEO makes one hundred times

more than the average worker than if the CEO makes ten times more, but even so, the real income of both will have become commensurate with productivity.

10. See Economic Policy Institute, "Datazone," hourly wage decile cutoffs for workers from 1973 to 2005 (in 2005 dollars), which show the 90/10 ratio of hourly wages rising from 1979 to 1987, then drifting slowly upward. The differential of college graduates over high school graduates drops from 1973 to 1979 and then rises.

11. Ibid.

12. U.S. Bureau of the Census, *U.S. Statistical Abstract 2006*, table 632, and *U.S. Statistical Abstract 1982–1983*, table 671.

13. Tabulated from Economic Policy Institute, "Datazone," real hourly wage for all by education, 1973 to 2005 (in 2005 dollars).

14. Economic Policy Institute, "Datazone," hourly wage decile cutoffs for workers, 1973 to 2005 (in 2005 dollars).

15. There is an extensive literature examining the possible impact of technological change on inequality: see Autor, Katz, and Krueger, "Computing Inequality"; Acemoglu, "Technical Change, Inequality, and the Labor Market"; Levy and Murnane, "With What Skills Are Computers a Complement?"; Mishel and Bernstein, "Technology and the Wage Structure."

16. Freeman, "Labor Market Institutions and Earnings Inequality."

17. CNNMoney.com, "Wal-Mart Calls for Minimum Wage Hike."

18. Borjas, Freeman, and Katz, "On the Labor Market Effects of Immigration and Trade."

19. Poverty statistics are from Freeman, "The Rising Tide Lifts . . .?" (2002), updated from U.S. Bureau of the Census, *Historical Poverty Tables*, table 1.

20. Federman et al., "What Does It Mean to Be Poor in America?"

21. Freeman, "The Rising Tide Lifts . . .?" (2002).

22. Federman et al., "What Does It Mean to Be Poor in America?" Table 2 reports that poor families spent 66.1 percent of their average income of $11,596 on the three specified items (food, shelter, utilities). They spent 5.1 percent on apparel, 10.3 percent on transportation, and 2.8 percent on health care.

23. A comparison of thirteen countries in the Luxembourg Income Study (LIS) shows that the United States ranked next to last in the income of children in the tenth decile of living standards but was number one in the income of children in the ninetieth decile. See Rainwater and Smeeding, "Doing Poorly."

24. Freeman, "The Rising Tide Lifts . . .?" (2002).
25. Ibid.

Chapter 4

1. OECD, *Employment Outlook 2006*, table F. The European number is the median of the advanced European countries.
2. Ibid., table F for 2004. Koreans worked 2,394 hours over the year, and Americans worked 1,808 hours over the year.
3. Daume, "Gender Differences in Taking Vacation Time," tables 1 and 3.
4. U.S. Department of Labor, "Work at Home in 2004."
5. Freeman, "Working for Nothing."
6. Ibid.
7. Ibid.
8. ILO News, "Americans Work Longest Hours Among Industrialized Countries," September 6, 1999, was picked up by many U.S. newspapers; see http://www.hartford-hwp.com/archives/26/077.html.
9. Bjorklund and Freeman, "Searching for Optimal Inequality/Incentives."
10. Freeman and Schettkat, "Marketization of Household Production and the EU-U.S. Gap in Work," fig. 5.
11. Syracuse University, Campbell Public Affairs Institute, "Maxwell Poll," October 2006, 10.
12. Sousa-Poza and Henneberger, "Work Attitudes, Work Conditions, and Hours Constraints."
13. Shank, "Preferred Hours of Work and Corresponding Earnings." Full-time American workers want to work more than do full-time Europeans; see Reynolds, "When Too Much Is Not Enough."
14. Based on tabulations from census IPUMS; see Ruggles et al., *Integrated Public Use Microdata Series: Version 3.0.*
15. Bell and Freeman, "The Incentive for Working Hard."
16. Stier and Lewin-Epstein, "Time to Work."
17. Moldovanu and Sela, "The Optimal Allocation of Prizes in Contests."
18. For the details of the experiment, see Freeman and Gelber, "Optimal Inequality/Incentives: A Laboratory Experiment."
19. In many other countries, university administrators and government officials determine the number of places available for students in different fields, as the United States does in medical studies.
20. My first book, *The Market for College-Trained Manpower*, provides an

extensive assessment of student responsiveness from the 1950s and 1960s, including a large survey of student knowledge and attitudes.

21. Freeman, Chang, and Chiang, "Supporting 'the Best and Brightest' in Science and Engineering."
22. Kavita Shukla, undergraduate thesis, Cambridge, Mass.: Harvard University, 2005.
23. Preston, *Leaving Science.*

Chapter 5

1. U.S. Department of Labor, "Union Members in 2005," table 1, available at: http://www.bls.gov/news.release/union2.t01.htm.
2. For 2004, see ibid.; for 1990, see www.trinity.edu/bhirsch/union stats/. The rate in the private sector in North Carolina fell from 3.8 percent in 1990 to 2.1 percent in 2003.
3. Kauffman and Bennett, *What Do Unions Do? A Twenty-Year Perspective.*
4. Buhle, *Taking Care of Business.*
5. Freeman, "Why Are Unions Faring Poorly in NLRB Representation Elections?"
6. Dark, "Decline: The 1995 Race for the AFL-CIO Presidency."
7. On unionization by industry and occupation, see CPS data at "Union Membership and Coverage Database," www.trinity.edu/bhirsch/unionstats/. Riddell and Riddell (2003) find that at most 20 percent of the drop in union density from 1984 to 1998 was associated with shifts in the composition of employment by industry or occupation.
8. Data on unionization by demographic characteristics are tabulated from the MORG files available at NBER, "CPS Merged Outgoing Rotation Groups."
9. Schmidt and Zipperer (2007). In an earlier study, Brofenbrenner (2000) found that as many as 25 percent of *employers* facing a union drive fire at least one worker for union activity.
10. Freeman and Rogers, *What Workers Want,* 2nd ed., exhibit 3.8.
11. Bryson and Freeman, "Worker Needs and Voice in the U.S. and U.K."
12. Farber and Western, "Ronald Reagan and the Politics of Declining Union Organization"; Freeman and Rogers, "Open-Source Unionism."
13. Flanagan, "Has Management Strangled U.S. Unions?"; Farber, "Trends in Worker Demand for Union Representation"; McLennan, "A Management Perspective on *What Do Unions Do?*"

14. Freeman and Rogers, *What Workers Want*, 2nd ed.
15. Following up these results, Hart Research Associates asked workers in 1997, 1999, and 2001 about their desires for a non-union mode of meeting with management to discuss workplace issues and found a similar result; see Freeman and Rogers, *What Workers Want*, 2nd ed., introduction.
16. McLennan ("A Management Perspective on *What Do Unions Do?*") suggests that this might be the case for many respondents.
17. Doucouliagos and Laroche, "What Do Unions Do to Productivity?"
18. Freeman, "What Do Unions Do to Voting?"
19. Freeman, Boxall, and Haynes, *What Workers Say*.
20. Jolls, "The Role and Functioning of Public-Interest Legal Organizations in the Enforcement of the Employment Laws"; Kimberly and Freeman, *Can Labor Standards Improve Under Globalization?*
21. Osterman, *Gathering Power*; Fine, *Worker Centers*.
22. Freeman and Hersch, introduction to Freeman, Hersch, and Mishel, *Emerging Labor Market Institutions*.
23. Freeman, "Spurts in Union Growth."
24. The affiliates of the Communication Workers Union (CWU) are: Alliance@IBM, a minority union within IBM; Washington Alliance of Technology Workers, another Communication Workers affiliate based on IT workers in northern California and Washington; and the National Writers Union, an affiliate of the United Automobile Workers, which organizes freelance writers around the country. See Diamond and Freeman, "Will Unionism Prosper in Cyberspace?" The Communication Workers Union has expanded its effort to connect IT workers (www.techsunite.org) and developed a five-city organizing campaign associated with this website. The Machinists established CyberLodge (www.cyberlodge.org), and the Steelworkers initiated a "new form of individual membership—open to anyone regardless of employment," that offered modest services at modest dues.
25. See Working America, www.workingamerica.org.
26. Greenhouse, "Labor Federation Looks Beyond Unions."

Chapter 6

1. Freeman, "Decline of Labor Market Discrimination and Economic Analysis"; see also Freeman, "Changes in the Labor Market for Black Americans." I show how young blacks responded to the new opportunities to work in the U.S. business sector in *The Black Elite*.

2. In "Ranking Tables: United States and States: R1802: Percent of People 21 to 64 Years Old with a Disability: 2005 Universe," the U.S. Bureau of the Census reports a disability rate of 12.7 percent from the 2005 American Community Survey.
3. See EEOC, "Disability Discrimination."
4. See EEOC, "Charge Statistics, FY1992 Through FY2005."
5. Haveman, Halberstadt, and Burkhauser, *Public Policy Toward Disabled Workers*.
6. See Hotchkiss, *The Labor Market Experience of Workers with Disabilities*; Acemoglu and Angrist, "Consequences of Employment Protection?"; Beegle and Stock, "The Labor Market Effects of Disability Discrimination Laws."
7. Children's Defense Fund, "Edelman Decries President's Betrayal of Promise 'Not to Hurt Children,'" July 31, 1996.
8. U.S. Bureau of the Census, *U.S. Statistical Abstract 1978*, table 566.
9. Murray, *Losing Ground*.
10. Data from U.S. Department of Health and Human Services, "Temporary Assistance for Needy Families . . . Caseload Data."
11. Acs and Loprest, *Leaving Welfare*; Golden, "Welfare Reform Worked—Mostly."
12. U.S. Bureau of the Census, *U.S. Statistical Abstract 2006*, table 636.
13. The EITC is a tax credit for people who work and have earned income; see Greenstein, "The Earned Income Tax Credit."
14. Brown, Gilroy, and Cohen, "Time-Series Evidence of the Effect of the Minimum Wage on Youth Employment."
15. Card and Krueger, *Myth and Measurement*.
16. This is the theory of monopsony. In *Monopsony in Motion*, Alan Manning argues that economists have understated the importance of monopsony in the labor market.
17. EITC benefits chart available at: http://www.cbpp.org/eic2007/08_Benefits.pdf.
18. However, the taxes that fund the EITC are likely to reduce economic efficiency and impair employment creation. Thus, the gains in income transfer and employment from the EITC must be balanced against the costs due to taxes.
19. Data on Social Security administrative expenses are from Social Security and Medicare Boards of Trustees, "Status of the Social Security and Medicare Programs: A Summary of the 2006 Annual Reports." Expenses for private accounts can vary; some countries with private accounts place a limit on those expenses as a proportion of expenditures.

Notes

20. See U.S. Social Security Administration, "Report of the National Com-
    mission on Social Security Reform"; and 1994–96 Advisory Council
    Report, "Findings, Recommendations, and Statements." For a detailed
    discussion of the debate over the Bush proposals, see Wikipedia,
    "Social Security Debate, United States," http://en.wikipedia
    .org/wiki/Social_Security_debate_%28United_States%29#endnote_
    www.guardian.co.uk.961.
21. Various economists have developed plans to treat the transition cost
    problem; see ibid.
22. For the Australian plan, see Wikipedia, "Superannuation in Aus-
    tralia," http://en.wikipedia.org/wiki/Superannuation_in_Australia.
    For the Swedish system, see Turner, "Private Accounts in Sweden";
    and Normann and Mitchell, "Pension Reform in Sweden." For the
    Swiss plan, see James, "Reforming Social Security."
23. See Pensions Commission, "A New Pension Settlement for the
    Twenty-first Century."
24. Gold, "Risk Transfer in Public Pension Plans."
25. Congressional Budget Office, "Evaluating Benefit Guarantees in So-
    cial Security."
26. In 1998 I organized a forum to bring together economists favorable to
    privatization and those opposed to privatization with trade union
    leaders. The education director of the AFL-CIO helped plan the meet-
    ing and arranged for it to be held at a venue in Washington, D.C. But
    the weekend before the Social Security discussion was scheduled to
    take place, top AFL-CIO leaders suddenly announced that they were
    canceling the space and told the union folks that the event was off.
    Holding an open discussion on an issue with all sides presenting
    their views was fine for academia but not for trade unionists. The
    AFL-CIO leadership operated by giving "marching orders" to union
    activists. They did not want activists to engage in intellectual dis-
    course with persons who disagreed with official views. Given the
    risks and problems with privatization, they had no reason to fear
    open discussion, but they did.
27. This is sometimes called the first law of public finance. For my first
    and second laws of earnings dispersion, see page 46.
28. The percentage decline in the Gini coefficient for the United States is
    smaller than that for all but two of the other countries, Italy and
    Switzerland; see Bradley et al., "Distribution and Redistribution in
    Postindustrial Democracies," table 2.
29. OECD data ("Chart 1: Change in Health Expenditure . . ."), show that

the United States spends 15.3 percent of GDP on health compared to 8.9 percent for the average OECD country.

30. Appelbaum and Freeman, "Instead of a Tax Cut, Send Out Dividends."

Chapter 7

1. Delphi statement on bankruptcy proceedings, October 9, 2005. Miller reduced his salary to $1 per year, effective January 1, 2006, continuing until Delphi emerged from its reorganization in Chapter 11. The U.S. bankruptcy court approved a multimillion-dollar bonus plan for top Delphi Corporation executives in 2006.

2. It was Wilson's character Geraldine who excused anything that she had done that she shouldn't have done with the phrase "The Devil made me do it"; see http://www.quotationspage.com/quote/38014.html.

3. See the Employee Assistance Program Directory at http://www.eap-sap.com.

4. The Wal-Mart memo, "Reviewing and Revising Wal-Mart's Benefits Strategy," is available at: http://walmartwatch.com/img/site stream/docs/Susan_Chambers_Memo_to_Wal-Mart_Board.pdf.

5. See Bernstein, Bivens, and Dube for one analysis of what would happen to Wal-Mart if it had to pay 20 percent higher labor costs.

6. Greenhouse and Barbaro, "Wal-Mart to Add More Part-timers and Wage Caps."

7. This does not mean that improving standards is easy; see Locke, Qin, and Brause, "Does Monitoring Improve Labor Standards?"

8. Freeman, "Can the U.S. Clear the Market for Representation and Participation?"

9. Ibid.

10. Bryson and Freeman, "Worker Needs and Voice in the U.S. and U.K."

11. Bartel et al., "Can a Work Organization Have an Attitude Problem?"

12. Freeman and Rogers, *What Workers Want*, 2nd ed., exhibit 3.9.

13. The arbitrator would have to have exceeded his or her authority, engaged in fraud or corruption, or violated basic due process for a court to overturn the decision. This is known as the Steelworkers Trilogy. See Stone, "The Steelworkers Trilogy and the Evolution of Labor Arbitration."

14. This is the *Circuit City Stores v. Adams* case. The Court held that virtually all employment agreements are subject to the Federal Arbitration

Act, a 1925 law that established procedures for arbitration in cases filed in federal court. The Supreme Court also reaffirmed an earlier decision that this act preempts state laws that bar or limit employers' ability to mandate arbitration of employment claims.

15. See U.S. Department of Labor, "Health Plans and Benefits: ERISA."
16. Based on private communication from Larry Beeferman, Shareholding 101106.doc. Beeferman uses flow-of-fund data, together with other sources, to obtain these estimates.
17. Bader and Gold, "Reinventing Pension Actuarial Science."
18. Based on Henry J. Kaiser Family Foundation, *Health Insurance Coverage in America: 2004 Data Update*, 34, table 9. Eighty-one percent of persons with family income at 200 percent of the poverty level or higher had employer-provided insurance, compared to 34.1 percent of those with family income below that level. The 1987 figure is from Cutler, "Employee Costs and the Decline in Health Insurance Coverage."
19. From September 30, 1996, the date when Disney CEO Michael Eisner received a stock option grant of 24 million shares (split-adjusted), through August 30, 2002, Eisner received compensation exceeding $700 million and Disney shareholders lost 22.6 percent of their investment. Over the same period, the Standard & Poor's 500 index gained 45.1 percent and the Standard & Poor's Entertainment and Leisure Index rose 46.4 percent.
20. The shareholders went to court against this huge severance pay. The Delaware court ruled that Disney management had not done anything wrong in making such a contract. Business can make bad decisions. See Chase, "Court Upholds Disney-Ovitz Decision."
21. Colvin, "The Great CEO Pay Heist"; PBS, "Commentary: Examining the Stock Option Scandal."
22. The 262-to-1 estimate is from Mishel, "Economic Snapshots." The 431-to-1 estimate is from United for a Fair Economy and Institute for Policy Studies, "CEO:Worker Pay Ratio Shoots Up to 431:1." See also Sahadi, "CEO Pay: Sky High Gets Even Higher."
23. DeCarlo, "Special Report: CEO Compensation."
24. Conyon and Murphy, "The Prince and the Pauper."
25. How do such practices reduce the incentive effect of options? Managers become less concerned about the company doing badly for a while because it may be easier for them to earn options from a lower value.
26. Saul, "Study Finds Backdating of Options Widespread"; Heron and

Lie, "Does Backdating Explain the Stock Price Pattern Around Executive Stock Option Grants?"

27. For a discussion of these reforms, see Clark, "Corporate Governance Changes in the Wake of the Sarbanes-Oxley Act."
28. See, for instance, Gabaiz and Landier, "Why Has CEO Pay Increased So Much?" For an analysis of the linkage between executive pay and manipulation of earnings, see Crocker and Slemrod, "The Economics of Earnings Manipulation and Managerial Compensation."
29. Lazear and Rosen, "Rank-Order Tournaments as Optimum Labor Contracts."
30. Blasi, Kruse, and Freeman, "Shared Capitalism at Work."
31. Kruse, *Profit Sharing*; Blasi, Kruse, and Bernstein, *In the Company of Owners*.
32. Freeman, Kruse, and Blasi, "Worker Responses to Shirking."
33. Freeman et al., "Creating a Bigger Pie?"

Chapter 8

1. Freeman, "The Great Doubling"; Freeman, "What Really Ails Europe (and America)."
2. Freeman, "The Great Doubling."
3. Labor calculated from International Labor Office (ILO) data at LABORSTA Internet, "Economically Active Populations Estimates and Projections, 2000"; capital calculated from Penn World Tables, as described in Freeman, "The Great Doubling"; figures scaled so that the capital-to-labor ratio before the entry of China, India, and the ex-Soviet bloc is 1.00.
4. Harvard Law School, "The Ending of Global Textile Quotas."
5. World Bank, "World Development Indicators," table 4.9.
6. The 1990s growth in China did little, however, to advance the economic position of peasants. The rising inequality and the lack of political freedom and of legitimate channels of protest present a challenge to China and to the transition process. There is a danger that if and when the economy runs into economic problems, one outcome might be social disorder on a scale that reduces growth prospects. The Chinese government has developed some policies to address the inequality problem, but it continues to outlaw independent unions, which it fears would threaten the Communist Party monopoly on power.

7. Here are some average hourly cost figures that make this point:

Average Hourly Labor Cost in Textile Industry

Turkey	$2.13
Peru	1.63
Mexico	2.30
South Africa	2.17
Bangladesh	0.25
Sri Lanka	0.40
China—inland	0.41
China—coastal	0.69

8. For discussions of the Washington consensus, see Wikipedia, "Washington Consensus," http://en.wikipedia.org/wiki/Washington_ Consensus.
9. OECD 2005.
10. To find out how many graduates in developing countries are candidates for jobs in multinational firms, in 2005 the McKinsey Global Institute asked recruiters for multinationals what proportion of graduates from developing and transition economies they viewed as good candidates for jobs. The recruiters came up with numbers ranging from 10 to 20 percent, depending on the occupation and country. Strong English-language skills were a key factor; many of the workers whom the multinationals did not feel met their requirements could undoubtedly do world-class work for firms in their own countries and languages. But even 10 to 20 percent of an increasing number of graduates from developing countries adds immensely to the supply pool from which multinationals fill vacancies.
11. Freeman, "Does Globalization of the Scientific/Engineering Workforce Threaten U.S. Economic Leadership?"
12. Krugman, "A Model of Innovation, Technology Transfer, and the World Distribution of Income"; Gomory and Baumol, *Global Trading and Conflicting National Interests*.
13. Samuelson, "Where Ricardo and Mill Rebut and Confirm Arguments of Mainstream Economists Supporting Globalization."
14. Bhagwati, Panagariya, and Srinivasan, "The Muddles over Outsourcing."
15. Freeman, "Does Globalization of the Scientific/Engineering Workforce Threaten U.S. Economic Leadership?"
16. Institute of Directors, "Offshoring Is Here to Stay."

Chapter 9

1. Artificial agent models are computer game–type simulations in which the analyst specifies "goals" for the agents and means of attaining those goals. To the extent that the models capture parts of economic reality, they offer ways to assess the potential impact of policies. For a discussion of these models, see Epstein, "Remarks on the Foundations of Agent-Based Generative Social Science." For lots of additional information on these models, see Tesfatsion, "Agent-Based Computational Economics"; see also Wikipedia, "Agent Based Model," http://en.wikipedia.org/wiki/Agent_based_model. Because I believe this tool offers a fruitful way to assess labor reforms, I teach a course that covers it at Harvard, much to the surprise of my colleagues in the labor field, who think it is outré or slightly barmy.

2. See Wikipedia, "Paul Erdös," http://en.wikipedia.org/wiki/Paul_Erdos. Erdös traveled from one mathematics department to another around the world and supposedly would say, "My mind is open," when presented with whatever problems the local mathematicians needed help in solving.

3. The deadweight losses are generated by responsive economic behavior to avoid paying those taxes; see Wikipedia, "Deadweight Loss," http://en.wikipedia.org/wiki/Deadweight_loss.

4. For a detailed analysis of one policy I think would help the United States develop a stronger science and engineering workforce, see Freeman, "Supporting the Best and Brightest."

5. See Brainard, Litan, and Warren, "Insuring America's Workers in a New Era of Offshoring"; see also Kling, "Fundamental Restructuring of Unemployment Insurance: Wage-Loss Insurance and Temporary Earnings Replacement Accounts"; Kletzer and Rosen, "Reforming Unemployment Insurance for the Twenty-first Century Workforce"; Hacker, "Universal Insurance: Enhancing Economic Security to Promote Opportunity."

6. Utt, "The Bridge to Nowhere."

7. This is known as the Coase theorem of efficient bargaining. It says that parties to an economic transaction do not "leave money on the table." There are sufficient divergences from this behavior in the economy and even in game theory models that its application must be assessed carefully in any reform. See Freeman, "Searching for the EU Social Dialogue Model."

8. Freeman, "Will Labor Fare Better Under State Labor Relations Law?"

REFERENCES

Acemoglu, Daron. 2002. "Technical Change, Inequality, and the Labor Market." *Journal of Economic Literature* (American Economic Association) 40(1, March): 7–72.

Acemoglu, Daron, and Joshua Angrist. 2001. "Consequences of Employment Protection? The Case of the Americans with Disabilities Act." *Journal of Political Economy* 109(5): 915–57.

Ackman, Dan. 2002. "CEO for Life?" *Forbes*, April 25. Available at: http://www.forbes.com/2002/04/25/0425ceotenure.html.

Acs, Gregory, and Pamela Loprest. 2004. *Leaving Welfare: Employment and Well-being of Families That Left Welfare in the Post-Entitlement Era*. Kalamazoo, Mich.: W. E. Upjohn Institute.

Appelbaum, Eileen, and Richard Freeman. 2001. "Instead of a Tax Cut, Send Out Dividends." *New York Times*, Op-Ed, February 3.

Autor, David H., Lawrence F. Katz, and Alan B. Krueger. 1998. "Computing Inequality: Have Computers Changed the Labor Market?" *Quarterly Journal of Economics* 113(November): 1169–1213.

Bader, Lawrence N., and Jeremy Gold. n.d. "Reinventing Pension Actuarial Science." Available at: http://users.erols.com/jeremygold/reinventingpensionactuarialscience.pdf.

Bartel, Ann, Richard Freeman, Casey Ichniowski, and Morris M. Kleiner. 2003. "Can a Work Organization Have an Attitude Problem? The Impact of Workplaces on Employee Attitudes and Economic Outcomes." Working paper 9987. Cambridge, Mass.: National Bureau of Economic Research (September).

Beegle, Kathleen, and Wendy A. Stock. n.d. "The Labor Market Effects of Disability Discrimination Laws." Available at: http://www.montana.edu/stock/Beegle%20and%20Stock%20TEXT.PDF#search=%22disabled%20workers%20haveman%22.

Bell, Linda, and Richard B. Freeman. 2001. "The Incentive for Working Hard: Explaining Hours Worked Differences in the U.S. and Germany." *Labor Economics* 8(2, May): 181–202.

Bernstein, Jared, L., Josh Bivens, and Arindrajit Dube. 2006. "Wrestling with Wal-Mart: Tradeoffs Between Profits, Prices, and Wages," *Economic Policy Institute Working Paper*, June 15.

References

Bhagwati, Jagdish, Arvind Panagariya, and T. N. Srinivasan, 2004. "The Muddles over Outsourcing." *Journal of Economic Perspectives* 18(4): 93–114.

Bjorklund, Anders, and Richard Freeman. 2006. "Searching for Optimal Inequality/Incentives: Sweden's Effort to Reach Economic Valhalla." Unpublished paper (September).

Blasi, Joseph, Douglas Kruse, and Aaron Bernstein. 2003. *In the Company of Owners*. New York: HarperCollins.

Blasi, Joseph, Douglas Kruse, and Richard Freeman. 2006. "Shared Capitalism at Work: Impacts and Policy Options." In *America at Work: Choices and Challenges*, edited by Edward Lawler and James O'Toole. New York: Palgrave Macmillan.

Borjas, George, Richard Freeman, and Lawrence Katz. 1991. "On the Labor Market Effects of Immigration and Trade." Working paper 3761. Cambridge, Mass.: National Bureau of Economic Research (June).

Botero, Juan, Simeon Djankov, Rafael Porta, and Florencio C. Lopez-De-Silanes. 2004. "The Regulation of Labor." *Quarterly Journal of Economics* (MIT Press) 119(4, November): 1339–82.

Bradley, David, Evelyne Huber, Stephanie Moller, François Nielsen, and John D. Stephens. 2003. "Distribution and Redistribution in Postindustrial Democracies." *World Politics* 55(2, January): 193–228.

Brainard, Lael, Robert E. Litan, and Nicholas Warren. 2005. "Insuring America's Workers in a New Era of Offshoring." Brookings Institution policy brief 143 (July). Available at: http://www.brook.edu/comm/policybriefs/pb143.pdf.

Bronfenbrenner, Kate. 2000. *Uneasy Terrain: The Impact of Capital Mobility on Workers, Wages, and Union Organizing*. Washington: Trade Deficit Review Commission.

Brown, Charles, Curtis Gilroy, and Andrew Cohen. 1983. "Time-Series Evidence of the Effect of the Minimum Wage on Youth Employment." *Journal of Human Resources* 18(1, Winter): 3–31.

Bryson, Alex, and Richard Freeman. 2006. "Worker Needs and Voice in the U.S. and U.K." Working paper 12310. Cambridge, Mass.: National Bureau of Economic Research (June).

Buhle, Paul. 1999. *Taking Care of Business: Samuel Gompers, George Meany, Lane Kirkland, and the Tragedy of American Labor*. New York: Monthly Review Press.

Camarota, Steven A. 2004. "A Jobless Recovery? Immigrant Gains and Native Losses" (October). Available at: Center for Immigration Studies, http://www.cis.org/articles/2004/back1104.pdf.

Card, David, and Alan Krueger. 1997. *Myth and Measurement: The New Economics of the Minimum Wage.* Princeton, N.J.: Princeton University Press.

Central Intelligence Agency (CIA). n.d. "Field Listing: Distribution of Family Income: Gini Coefficient." In *The World Factbook,* available at: https://www.cia.gov/cia/publications/factbook/fields/2172.html.

Chase, Randall. 2006. "Court Upholds Disney-Ovitz Decision." Associated Press, June 8.

Chi, Wei, Richard Freeman, and Morris Kleiner. 2005. "Does Voluntary Job Changing Improve Work Satisfaction?" SOLE/EALE (Society of Labor Economics/European Association of Labour Economists) tenth annual meetings. San Francisco (June 2–5).

Chor, Davin, and Richard Freeman. 2005. "The 2004 Global Labor Survey: Workplace Institutions and Practices Around the World." Working paper 11598. Cambridge, Mass.: National Bureau of Economic Research (September).

Clark, Robert. Forthcoming. "Corporate Governance Changes in the Wake of the Sarbanes-Oxley Act: A Morality Tale for Policymakers Too." *Georgia State University Law Review.*

CNNMoney.com. 2005. "Wal-Mart Calls for Minimum Wage Hike" (October 25). Available at: http://money.cnn.com/2005/10/25/news/fortune500/walmart_wage/.

Columbia University. Clearinghouse on International Developments in Child, Youth, and Family Policies. 2001. "U.S. Unemployment Insurance: A Safety Net with Holes" (December). Available at: http://www.childpolicyintl.org/issuebrief/issuebrief3pdf.pdf#search=%22unemployment%20benefits%20replacement%20rates%20us%20%22.

Colvin, Geoffrey. 2001. "The Great CEO Pay Heist." *Fortune,* June 25.

Congressional Budget Office. 2006. "Evaluating Benefit Guarantees in Social Security." Background paper (March). Available at: http://www.cbo.gov/ftpdocs/70xx/doc7058/03-07-SS_Guarantees.pdf.

Conyon, Martin J., and Kevin J. Murphy. 2000. "The Prince and the Pauper: CEO Pay in the United States and United Kingdom." *Economic Journal* 110(467, November): F640–71.

Council of Economic Advisers. Various years. *Economic Report of the President.* Washington: U.S. Government Printing Office.

Crocker, Keith J., and Joel Slemrod. 2006. "The Economics of Earnings Manipulation and Managerial Compensation." Working paper 12645. Cambridge, Mass.: National Bureau of Economic Research (October).

Cutler, David. 2002. "Employee Costs and the Decline in Health Insurance

Coverage." Working paper 9036. Cambridge, Mass.: National Bureau of Economic Research (July).

Dark, Taylor E. 1999. "Decline: The 1995 Race for the AFL-CIO Presidency—American Federation of Labor and Congress of Industrial Organizations." *Labor History* 40(3): 323–43.

Daume, David. 2006. "Gender Differences in Taking Vacation Time." *Work and Occupations* 33(2, May): 161–90.

DeCarlo, Scott, ed. 2005. "Special Report: CEO Compensation." *Forbes*, April 21. Available at: http://www.forbes.com/2005/04/20/05ceoland.html.

Devroye, Dan, and Richard Freeman. 2001. "Does Inequality of Skills Explain Inequality of Earnings Across Advanced Countries?" Working paper 8140. Cambridge, Mass.: National Bureau of Economic Research (February).

Dew-Becker, Ian, and Robert J. Gordon. 2005. "Where Did the Productivity Growth Go? Inflation Dynamics and the Distribution of Income." Working paper 11842. Cambridge, Mass.: National Bureau of Economic Research (December).

Diamond, Wayne J., and Richard B. Freeman. 2002. "Will Unionism Prosper in Cyberspace? The Promise of the Internet for Employee Organization." *British Journal of Industrial Relations* (Blackwell Publishers/London School of Economics) 40(3): 569–96.

Doucouliagos, Chris (Hristos), and Patrice Laroche. 2003. "What Do Unions Do to Productivity? A Meta-Analysis." *Industrial Relations* 42(October): 650–91.

Economic Policy Institute. n.d. "Datazone: Mean Family Income by Quintile and Top 5%, 1966–2003 (2003 Dollars)." Available at: http://www.epi.org/datazone/06/inc_by_fifth.pdf.

Epstein, Joshua M. 2005. "Remarks on the Foundations of Agent-Based Generative Social Science." CSED working paper 41. Washington, D.C.: Brookings Institution, Center on Social and Economic Dynamics (July). Available at: http://www.brook.edu/es/dynamics/papers/csed_wp41.htm.

European Commission. 2006. "European Year of Workers' Mobility 2006: Facts and Figures." Available at: http://ec.europa.eu/employment_social/workersmobility_2006/index.cfm?id_page_category=FF.

Evans, John M., Douglas C. Lippoldt, and Pascal Marianna. 2001. "Trends in Working Hours in OECD Countries." *OECD Labour Market and Social Policy Occasional Papers*, No. 45. Available at: http://caliban.sourceoecd.org/vl=9395500/cl=16/nw=1/rpsv/cgi-bin/wppdf?file=5lgsjhvj7rs5.pdf

Farber, Henry S. 1989. "Trends in Worker Demand for Union Representation." *American Economic Review* (papers and proceedings of the 101st meeting) 70(2): 166–71.

Farber, Henry S., and Bruce Western. 2002. "Ronald Reagan and the Politics of Declining Union Organization," *British Journal of Industrial Relations* 40(3): 385–401.

Federman, Maya, Thesia I. Garner, Kathleen Short, W. Boman Cutter IV, John Kiely, David Levine, Duane McDough, and Marilyn McMillen. 1996. "What Does It Mean to Be Poor in America?" *Monthly Labor Review* 119(5, May): 3–17.

Fine, Janice. 2006. *Worker Centers: Organizing Communities at the Edge of the Dream*. Ithaca, N.Y.: Cornell University/ILR Press.

Flanagan, Robert J. 2005. "Has Management Strangled U.S. Unions?" *Journal of Labor Research* 26(1): 33–63.

Freeman, Richard B. 1971. *The Market for College-Trained Manpower*. Cambridge, Mass.: Harvard University Press.

———. 1973. "Changes in the Labor Market for Black Americans." *Brookings Papers* (Summer).

———. 1973. "Decline of Labor Market Discrimination and Economic Analysis." *American Economic Review* 63(2, May): 280–86.

———. 1976. *The Black Elite: The New Market for Highly Educated Black Americans*. New York: McGraw-Hill.

———. 1976. *The Overeducated American*. New York: Academic Press.

———. 1985. "Why Are Unions Faring Poorly in NLRB Representation Elections?" In *Challenges and Choices Facing American Labor*, edited by Tom Kochan. Cambridge, Mass.: MIT Press.

———. 1994. "How Labor Fares in Advanced Countries." In Richard B. Freeman, *Working Under Different Rules*. New York: Russell Sage Foundation.

———. 1994. *Working Under Different Rules*. New York and Cambridge, Mass.: Russell Sage Foundation and National Bureau of Economic Relations.

———. 1996. "Labor Market Institutions and Earnings Inequality." *New England Economic Review: Spatial and Labor Market Contributions to Earnings Inequality* (Federal Reserve Bank of Boston) (May–June): 157–68.

———. 1997. "Working for Nothing: The Supply of Volunteer Labor." *Journal of Labor Economics* 15: S140–66.

———. 1998. "Spurts in Union Growth: Defining Moments and Social Processes." In *The Defining Moment: The Great Depression and the American Economy in the Twentieth Century*, edited by Michael Bordo, Claudia

171

References

Goldin, and Eugene White. Chicago: University of Chicago Press/National Bureau of Economic Research.

———. 1998. "War of the Models: Which Labor Market Institutions for the Twenty-first Century?" *Labor Economics* 5: 1–24.

———. 2002. "The Rising Tide Lifts . . .?" In *Understanding Poverty*, edited by Sheldon Danziger and Robert Haveman. Cambridge, Mass.: Harvard University Press.

———. 2003. "Varieties of Labor Market Institutions and Economic Performance." Paper presented to the Industrial Relations and Research Association (IRRA) session on "Labor Market Institutions and Economic Outcomes." (January 4).

———. 2003. "What Do Unions Do to Voting?" Working paper 9992. Cambridge, Mass.: National Bureau of Economic Research (September).

———. 2005. "The Great Doubling: America in the New Global Economy." Usery Lecture, Georgia State University (April 8).

———. 2005. "What Really Ails Europe (and America): The Doubling of the Global Workforce." *The Globalist*, June 3. Available at: http://www.theglobalist.com/StoryId.aspx?StoryId=4542.

———. 2006. "Does Globalization of the Scientific/Engineering Workforce Threaten U.S. Economic Leadership?" In *Innovation Policy and the Economy*, edited by Adam Jaffe, Joshua Lerner, and Scott Stern. 6: 123–58.

———. 2006. "People Flows in Globalization." *Journal of Economic Perspective* 20(2, Summer): 145–70.

———. 2006. "Supporting the Best and Brightest." Washington, D.C.: Brookings Institution, Hamilton Project (December).

———. 2006. "Will Labor Fare Better Under State Labor Relations Law?" Labor and Employment Relations Association (LERA) meetings. Boston, MA (January 7th).

———. Forthcoming. "Can the U.S. Clear the Market for Representation and Participation?" In *What Workers Say: Employee Voice in the Anglo-American World*, edited by Richard Freeman, Peter Boxall, and Peter Haynes. Ithaca, N.Y.: Cornell University Press.

Freeman, Richard B., Peter Boxall, and Peter Haynes, eds. Forthcoming. *What Workers Say: Employee Voice in the Anglo-American World*. Ithaca, N.Y.: Cornell University Press.

Freeman, Richard, Tanwin Chang, and Hanley Chiang 2005. "Supporting 'the Best and Brightest' in Science and Engineering: NSF Graduate Research Fellowships." Working paper 11623. Cambridge, Mass.: National Bureau of Economic Research (September).

Freeman, Richard, and Alex Gelber. 2006. "Optimal Inequality/Incentives: A Laboratory Experiment." Working paper 12588. Cambridge, Mass.: National Bureau of Economic Research (October).

Freeman, Richard, and Joni Hersch. 2005. Introduction to *Emerging Labor Market Institutions for the Twenty-first Century*, edited by Richard B. Freeman, Joni Hersch, and Lawrence Mishel. Chicago: University of Chicago Press.

Freeman, Richard, Douglas Kruse, and Joseph Blasi. 2006. "Worker Responses to Shirking." Paper presented at National Bureau of Economic Research conference on "Shared Capitalism." Russell Sage Foundation, New York, NY (October 5).

Freeman, Richard, Douglas Kruse, Joseph Blasi, and Chris Makin. 2006. "Creating a Bigger Pie? The Effects of Employee Ownership, Profit Sharing, and Stock Options on Workplace Performance." Paper presented at National Bureau of Economic Research conference on "Shared Capitalism." (October 5).

Freeman, Richard B., and James L. Medoff. 1984. *What Do Unions Do?* New York: Basic Books.

Freeman, Richard B., and Joel Rogers. 2002. "Open-Source Unionism: Beyond Exclusive Collective Bargaining." *WorkingUSA: The Journal of Labor and Society* 7(2): 3–4. Available at: http://www.workingusa.org.

———. 2006. *What Workers Want*, 2nd ed. Ithaca, N.Y.: Cornell University Press.

Freeman, Richard, and Ronald Schettkat. 2005. "Marketization of Household Production and the EU-U.S. Gap in Work." *Economic Policy* 20(41): 6–50.

Gabaiz, Xavier, and Augustin Landier. 2006. "Why Has CEO Pay Increased So Much?" Working paper 12365. Cambridge, Mass.: National Bureau of Economic Research (July). Available at: http://www.nber.org/papers/w12365.

Gold, Jeremy. 2003. "Risk Transfer in Public Pension Plans." In The Pension Challenge: Risk Transfers and Retirement Income Security, edited by Olivia S. Mitchell and Kent Smetters. New York: Oxford University Press.

Golden, Olivia. 2006. "Welfare Reform Worked—Mostly." *Mother Jones*, July 28. Available at: http://www.motherjones.com/commentary/columns/2006/07/welfare_reform.html.

Gomory, Ralph, and William J. Baumol. 2000. *Global Trading and Conflicting National Interests*. Cambridge, Mass.: MIT Press.

Greenhouse, Steven. 2004. "Labor Federation Looks Beyond Unions." *New York Times*, July 11.

References

Greenhouse, Steven, and Michael Barbaro. 2006. "Wal-Mart to Add More Part-timers and Wage Caps." *New York Times,* October 2.

Greenhouse, Steven, and David Leonhard. 2006. "Real Wages Fail to Match a Rise in Productivity. *New York Times,* August 28.

Greenstein, Robert. 2005. "The Earned Income Tax Credit: Boosting Employment, Aiding the Working Poor." Available at: Center on Budget Policy and Priorities, http://www.cbpp.org/7-19-05eic.htm.

Gwartney, James, and Robert Lawson. 2006. "Economic Freedom of the World: 2006 Annual Report." Available at: Fraser Institute, www.freetheworld.com/2006/IEFW2006ch1.pdf.

Hacker, Jacob S. 2006. "Universal Insurance: Enhancing Economic Security to Promote Opportunity" (September). Available at: Hamilton Project, http://www1.hamiltonproject.org/es/hamilton/hamilton_hp.htm.

Harris Poll. (Louis Harris Poll). 1984.

Hart Research Associates (Peter D. Hart Research Associates). 1993–2005.

Harvard Law School. Labor and Worklife Program. 2005. "The Ending of Global Textile Quotas: Understanding the New Shape of the World Economy." Conference at Harvard Law School (May 23–24) (briefing book available from Labor and Worklife Program).

Haveman, Robert H., Victor Halberstadt, and Richard V. Burkhauser. 1985. *Public Policy Toward Disabled Workers: Cross-national Analyses of Economic Impacts.* Ithaca, N.Y.: Cornell University Press.

Heron, Randall A., and Erik Lie. Forthcoming. "Does Backdating Explain the Stock Price Pattern Around Executive Stock Option Grants?" *Journal of Financial Economics.*

Hirsch, Barry T., and David A. Macpherson, "Union Membership and Coverage Database from the Current Population Survey: Note," *Industrial and Labor Relations Review* 56(2, January): 349–54. Available at: http://www.trinity.edu/bhirsch/unionstats/.

Hotchkiss, Julie L. 2003. *The Labor Market Experience of Workers with Disabilities: The ADA and Beyond.* Kalamazoo, Mich.: W. E. Upjohn Institute.

Institute of Directors. 2006. "Offshoring Is Here to Stay" (January 23). Available at: http://www.politics.co.uk/issueoftheday/institute-direc-tors-offshoring-here-stay-$370499$367012.htm.

James, Estelle. 2005. "Reforming Social Security: Lessons from Thirty Countries." NCPA study 277 (June). Available at: National Center for Policy Analysis, http://www.ncpa.org/pub/st/st277/.

Jolls, Christine. 2005. "The Role and Functioning of Public-Interest Legal Organizations in the Enforcement of the Employment Laws." In *Emerging Labor Market Institutions for the Twenty-first Century,* edited by

Richard B. Freeman, Joni Hersch, and Lawrence Mishel. Chicago: University of Chicago Press.

Jones, Del. 2006. "Forbes 400 Richest Americans Are All Billionaires This Year." *USA Today*, September 22.

Kaiser Family Foundation. Henry J. Kaiser Commission on Medicaid and the Uninsured. 2005. *Health Insurance Coverage in America: 2004 Data Update* (November). Available at: http://www.kff.org/uninsured/upload/Health-Coverage-in-America-2004-Data-Update-Report.pdf.

Kauffman, James T., and Bruce E. Bennett, eds. 2007. *What Do Unions Do? A Twenty-Year Perspective*. New Brunswick, N.J.: Transaction Publishers.

Keely, Louise C. 2005. "American Exceptionalism" (March). Available at: http://www.ssc.wisc.edu/~lkeely/americanexceptionalism.pdf.

Kimberly, Elliott, and Richard Freeman. 2003. *Can Labor Standards Improve Under Globalization?* Washington, D.C.: Institute for International Economics (June).

Kletzer, Lori G., and Howard Rosen. 2006. "Reforming Unemployment Insurance for the Twenty-first Century Workforce" (September). Available at: Hamilton Project, http://www1.hamiltonproject.org/es/hamilton/hamilton_hp.htm.

Kling, Jeffrey R. 2006. "Fundamental Restructuring of Unemployment Insurance: Wage-Loss Insurance and Temporary Earnings Replacement Accounts" (September). Available at: Hamilton Project, http://www1.hamiltonproject.org/es/hamilton/hamilton_hp.htm.

Krugman, Paul. 1979. "A Model of Innovation, Technology Transfer, and the World Distribution of Income." *Journal of Political Economy* 87: 253–66.

Kruse, Douglas. 1993. *Profit Sharing: Does It Make a Difference?* Kalamazoo, Mich.: W. E. Upjohn Institute.

LABORSTA Internet. 2000. "Economically Active Populations Estimates and Projections, 2000." Available at: laborsta.ilo.org.

Lalli, Gina. 2006. "The Effects of Day Care on Children's Emotional, Cognitive, and Social Development." *Perspectives* (University of New Hampshire) (Spring). Available at: www.unh.edu/sociology/Perspectives/Spring_2006/articles/Lalli_DayCare.pdf.

Lazear, Edward P., and Sherwin Rosen. 1981. "Rank-Order Tournaments as Optimum Labor Contracts." *Journal of Political Economy* 89(5, October): 841–64.

Levy, Frank, and Richard J. Murnane. 1996. "With What Skills Are Computers a Complement?" *American Economic Review* (American Economic Association) 86(2, May): 258–62.

References

Lipset, Seymour Martin. 1997. *American Exceptionalism: A Double-Edged Sword*. New York: Norton.

Locke, Richard, Fei Qin, and Alberto Brause. 2006. "Does Monitoring Improve Labor Standards? Lessons from Nike." MIT Sloan research paper 4612-06 (July).

Lombardi, Candace. 2006. "How to Marry a Billionaire? Start with Forbes List." *New York Times*, September 22.

Manning, Alan. 2003. *Monopsony in Motion*. Princeton, N.J.: Princeton University Press.

Martin, John P. 1994. "The Extent of High Unemployment in OECD Countries." Available at: http://www.kc.frb.org/Publicat/sympos/1994/S94MARTI.PDF.

McLennan, Kenneth. 2007. "A Management Perspective on *What Do Unions Do?*" In *What Do Unions Do? A Twenty-Year Perspective*, edited by James T. Kauffman and Bruce E. Bennett. New Brunswick, N.J.: Transaction Publishers.

Mishel, Lawrence. 2006. "Economic Snapshots: CEO-to-Worker Pay Imbalance Grows." (June 21). Available at: Economic Policy Institute, http://www.epinet.org/content.cfm/webfeatures_snapshots_20060621.

Mishel, Lawrence, and Jared Bernstein. 1998. "Technology and the Wage Structure: Has Technology's Impact Accelerated Since the 1970s?" *Research in Labor Economics* 17: 305–55.

Moldovanu, Benny, and Aner Sela. 2001. "The Optimal Allocation of Prizes in Contests." *American Economic Review* 91: 542–58.

Moscarini, Giuseppe, and Kaj Thomsson. 2006. "Occupational and Job Mobility in the United States." Yale Economic Applications and Policy Discussion Paper 19 (July). Available at: Social Science Research Network, http://papers.ssrn.com/sol3/papers.cfm?abstract_id=918072.

Murray, Charles. 1984. *Losing Ground: American Social Policy, 1950–1980*. New York: Basic Books.

Nasar, Sylvia. 1992. "Who Paid the Most Taxes in the 1980s: The Super Rich." *New York Times*, May 31.

National Academy of Sciences. 1995. *New Findings on Children, Families, and Economic Self-sufficiency: Summary of a Research Briefing*. Washington, D.C.: National Academies Press.

National Bureau of Economic Research. n.d. "CPS Merged Outgoing Rotation Groups," available at: http://www.nber.org/data/morg.html.

Normann, Goran, and Daniel J. Mitchell. 2000. "Pension Reform in Sweden: Lessons for American Policymakers." Backgrounder 1381 (June

29). Available at: Heritage Foundation, http://www.heritage.org/Research/SocialSecurity/bg1381.cfm.

Organization for Economic Cooperation and Development (OECD). Various years. *Employment Outlook*. Paris: OECD.

———. 2001. *Historical Statistics 1970–2000*. Paris: OECD.

———. 2005. Center for Education Research and Innovation, Education Database. Available at: http://www1.oecd.org/scripts/cde/members/linkpage.html

———. n.d. "Chart 1: Change in Health Expenditure as a Share of GDP, OECD Countries, 1990 and 2004." Available at: http://www.oecd.org/dataoecd/5/28/36992150.pdf.

Osawa, Machiko, and Jeff Kingston. 1996. "Flexibility and Inspiration: Restructuring and the Japanese Labor Market." *Japan Labor Bulletin: Special Topic* 35(1, January 1). Available at: http://www.jil.go.jp/bulletin/year/1996/vol35-01/04.htm.

Osterman, Paul. 2003. *Gathering Power: The Future of Progressive Politics in America*. Boston: Beacon Press.

Passell, Jeffrey S. 2006. "The Size and Characteristics of the Unauthorized Migrant Population in the U.S.: Estimates Based on the March 2005 Current Population Survey" (March 7). Available at: Pew Hispanic Center, http://pewhispanic.org/files/reports/61.pdf.

Pensions Commission. 2005. "A New Pension Settlement for the Twenty-first Century: The Second Report of the Pensions Commission." Available at: http://www.pensionscommission.org.uk/publications/2005/annrep/main-report.pdf#search=%22Turner%20commission%20report%22.

Phillips, Deborah A., and Anne Bridgman. 1995. *New Findings on Children, Families, and Economic Self-Sufficiency*. Washington, D.C.: National Academy Press.

Preston, Anne. 2004. *Leaving Science: Occupational Exit from Scientific Careers*. New York: Russell Sage Foundation.

Public Broadcasting System. 2006. "Commentary: Examining the Stock Option Scandal." *Nightly Business Report*, August 3. Available at: http://www.pbs.org/nbr/site/onair/transcripts/060803d.

Rainwater, Lee, and Timothy M. Smeeding. 1995. "Doing Poorly: The Real Income of American Children in Comparative Perspective." Luxembourg Income Study WP 127. Available at http://www.lisproject.org/publications/liswps/127.pdf.

Reynolds, Jeremy. 2004. "When Too Much Is Not Enough: Actual and Preferred Work Hours in the United States and Abroad." *Sociological Forum* 19(1, March): 89–120.

Riddell, Chris, and W. Craig Riddell. 2003. "Changing Patterns of Unionization: The North American Experience, 1984–1998," University of British Columbia, Department of Economics, September. Available at: http://www.econ.ubc.ca/ine/papers/wp007.pdf

Ruggles, Steven, Matthew Sobek, Trent Alexander, Catherine A. Fitch, Ronald Goeken, Patricia Kelly Hall, Miriam King, and Chad Ronnander. 2004. *Integrated Public Use Microdata Series: Version 3.0* (machine-readable database). Minneapolis: University of Minnesota, Minnesota Population Center (producer and distributor). Available at: http://www .ipums.org.

Sahadi, Jeanne. 2005. "CEO Pay: Sky High Gets Even Higher." CNN-Money.com, August 30. Available at: http://money.cnn.com/2005/ 08/26/news/economy/ceo_pay.

Samuelson, Paul A. 2004. "Where Ricardo and Mill Rebut and Confirm Arguments of Mainstream Economists Supporting Globalization." *Journal of Economic Perspectives* 18: 135–46.

Saul, Stephanie. 2006. "Study Finds Backdating of Options Widespread." *New York Times*, July 17.

Schmitt, John, and Ben Zipperer. 2007. "Dropping the Ax: Illegal Firings During Union Election Campaigns," Center for Economic and Policy Research Report, Washington, D.C. (January). Available at: http://www.cepr.net/index.php?option=com_content&task=view&id =775&Itemid=8.

Shank, Susan E. 1986. "Preferred Hours of Work and Corresponding Earnings." *Monthly Labor Review* 109(11, November): 40–44. Available at: http:// www.bls.gov/opub/mlr/1986/11/art8full.pdf.

Shukla, Kavita. 2006. "Varsity Science: A Study in the Factors that Affect Motivation Among Harvard Students and Influence Their Interest in Science, Arguing for a Science Education System Modeled on America's High School Athletic Programs." Undergraduate thesis. Cambridge, M.A.: Harvard University.

Simon, Herbert. 1965. *The Shape of Automation for Men and Management.* New York: Harper & Row.

Social Security and Medicare Boards of Trustees. 2006. "Status of the Social Security and Medicare Programs: A Summary of the 2006 Annual Reports" (May 2). Available at: http://www.ssa.gov/OACT/TRSUM/ trsummary.html.

Sousa-Poza, Alfonso, and Fred Henneberger. 2000. "Work Attitudes, Work Conditions, and Hours Constraints: An Explorative, Cross-national Analysis." *Labor* 14(3, September): 351–72.

Stier, Haya, and Noah Lewin-Epstein. 2003. "Time to Work: A Comparative Analysis of Preferences for Working Hours." *Work and Occupations* 30(3, August): 302–26.

Stone, Katherine V. W. 2005. "The Steelworkers Trilogy and the Evolution of Labor Arbitration." In *Labor Law Stories*, edited by Laura J. Cooper and Catherine L. Fisk. New York: Foundation Press. Available at: SSRN, http://ssrn.com/abstract=631343.

Tesfatsion, Leigh. 2006. "Agent-Based Computational Economics: Growing Economies from the Bottom Up." Available at: http://www.econ.iastate.edu/tesfatsi/ace.htm (last updated September 2, 2006).

Turner, John. 2005. "Private Accounts in Sweden" (March). Available at: AARP Public Policy Institute, http://www.aarp.org/research/legis-polit/ssreform/private_accounts_in_sweden.html.

Unionstats.com. n.d. "Union Membership and Coverage Database from the CPS." Available at: www.trinity.edu/bhirsch/unionstats.

United for a Fair Economy and Institute for Policy Studies. n.d. "CEO:Worker Pay Ratio Shoots Up to 431:1." Available at: http://www.faireconomy.org/press/2005/EE2005_pr.html.

U.S. Bureau of the Census. Various years. *The Statistical Abstract of the United States*. Available at: http://www.census.gov/compendia/statab/.

———. Various years. *Census Historical Poverty Tables*. Available at: http://www.census.gov/hhes/www/censpov.html.

———. 2005. *Current Population Survey: Annual Social and Economic (ASEC) Supplement*. Available at: http://www.census.gov/apsd/techdoc/cps/cpsmar05.pdf#search=%22CPS%20earnings%20topcode%202005%22.

U.S. Department of Commerce. Various years. *National Income and Product Accounts*. Available at: http://bea.gov/bea/dn/nipaweb/TableView.asp#Mid.

U.S. Department of Health and Human Services. Administration for Children and Families. Office of Family Assistance. Various years. "Temporary Assistance for Needy Families . . . Caseload Data." Available at: http://www.acf.hhs.gov/programs/ofa/caseload/caseloadindex.htm.

U.S. Department of Labor. n.d. "Health Plans and Benefits: ERISA," available at: http://www.dol.gov/dol/topic/health-plans/erisa.htm.

U.S. Department of Labor. Bureau of Labor Statistics. 2005. "Work at Home in 2004." USDL 05-1768 (September).

———. 2006. "Union Members in 2005." *News* USDL 06-99 (January 20).

U.S. Equal Employment Opportunity Commission. n.d. "Disability Discrimination." Available at: http://www.eeoc.gov/types/ada.html.

———. "Charge Statistics, FY1992 Through FY2005." Available at:

References

http://www.eeoc.gov/stats/charges.html (last updated January 27, 2006).

U.S. National Commission on Technology, Automation, and Economic Progress. 1966. *Technology and the American Economy*. Washington: U.S. Government Printing Office.

U.S. Social Security Administration. 1983. "Report of the National Commission on Social Security Reform" (January). Available at: http://www.ssa.gov/history/reports/gspan.html.

———. n.d. "1994–96 Advisory Council Report: Findings, Recommendations, and Statements." Available at: http://www.ssa.gov/history/reports/adcouncil/report/findings.htm#overview.

Utt, Ronald D. 2005. "The Bridge to Nowhere: A National Embarrassment." WebMemo 889 (October 20). Available at: Heritage Foundation, http://www.heritage.org/Research/Budget/wm889.cfm.

Viscusi, Kip. 1979. *Employment Hazards: An Investigation of Market Performance*. Harvard Economic Studies 148. Cambridge, Mass.: Harvard University Press.

Wikipedia. n.d. See http://en.wikipedia.org/.

World Bank. n.d. "World Development Indicators." Available at: http://devdata.worldbank.org/wdi2005/Section4.htm.

INDEX

Boldface numbers refer to figures and tables.

job mobility, 13–17
job satisfaction, 17
job security, 16
job-to-job mobility rate, 14
Journal of Labor Research, 76

Katz, L., 51
Kirkland, L., 77–78
Knights of Labor, 90
knowledge-based economy, 20
Korea: higher education, 70; investment in education, 133; work hours, 60
Krueger, A., 100
Kruse, D., 125

Labor and Worklife Program, Harvard Law School, 10, 150n4
labor law, 93, 147
labor market: and economic well-being of workers, 7; economists' views of, 3–4; employment rates, 20, 21–25; failure of, 20; Fraser indices, 8–10; globalization, 129–40; Global Labor Survey, 10; government regulation, 10, 17–19; as ideal market model, 19; immigrants in, 29–32; incentives for investment in education, 69–72; mobility of workers, 13–17; productivity and real wages, 33–40; share of national income, 37–38; in U.S. vs. other countries, 11–13, 18–19, 20; women in, 25–29; and workplace conditions, 109–10. *See also* unemployment
labor participation rates, of women, 25, 99

Latin America, growth of informal sector in, 131–32
Latin American immigrants, 29
lay offs, 13, 16
legal tradition, in U.S., 18
Lindsey, L., 153n27
litigation, 94, 96, 97, 117
living wages, 101, 113
Losing Ground (Murray), 98
Luxembourg Income Study (LIS), 155n23

managers and management: behavior determined by market conditions, 109–10; earnings of, 48; employees' ratings of, 85–86, 115; executive pay, 52, 119–24, 127; and unions, 80–82
Manning, A., 159n16
manufacturing, 152–53n24
Market for College-Trained Manpower (Freeman), 156n20
marketization, of household production, 28–29
markets, 46–47, 69–70, 109–10. *See also* labor market
mass transit systems, 146
maze experiment: inequality/incentives experiment, 66–69, 156n18
McKinsey Global Institute, 164n10
Meany, G., 77, 89
medical research, 31
Mexican immigrants, 29, 32
middle class, decline of, 49
migration, of workers within U.S., 14
Miller, S., 109
minimum wage, 17, 50–51, 100–101, 145